From the Well O' My Soul

LUSTER RAY LEWIS

From The Well O' My Soul
Author: Luster Ray Lewis

All rights reserved. No part of this book may be reproduced or transmitted in any form or by any means, electronic or mechanical, including photocopying, recording or by any information storage and retrieval system, without written permission from the producer, except for the inclusion of brief quotations in a review.

Copyright © 2019 by Marilyn K. Lewis
ISBN: 978-1-7321916-3-1
Library of Congress Control Number: 2019050088
Produced & Compiled by: Marilyn K. Lewis
Cover Design by: Paul Payne and Shanay Payne
Design & Layout by: Douglas DoNascimento

Published by:
    Briggs & Schuster
    BSA.IM

Printed in the United States of America

To My Dearest Luster

For whom I would not know the purest, most sincere love, were you not my renaissance man. You made a difference and have demonstrated selfless love and consummate passion for life.

Special Appreciation

Many thanks to devoted friends who have lovingly lent their talents and gifts to bring Luster's words to share. To Douglas DoNascimento for his willingness to bring a perpetual life to Luster's words. To Shanay and Paul Payne for their creative excellence and friendship to Luster and I creating the cover for our book. And finally to my beloved Luster for writing our story that others may learn the power of pure love.

The Author

Luster Ray Lewis

Born and raised in Dallas, TX Luster Ray Lewis was the first of four siblings. Luster served the US Air Force as a drill instructor and studied architecture at the University of Arlington. Described by many as a Renaissance Man, he was blessed with an analytical, mathematical, engineering, creative, artistic and poetic mind. Equipped with a patient and endearing personality, he understood how to give his full attention to someone and make them feel important. More than anything else, Luster had a desire to love and be loved.

All writings on this book were created by the author between 1999 and 2019.

From The Well O' My Soul

I was not emotionally prepared to part with Marilyn and admit to being shaken very deeply. I found that writing poetry to and about her soothed the extreme pain of losing the most wonderful woman that I have ever known. I felt as though I was communicating with her when I was writing. We both were very expressive about our feelings for each other. Writing seemed like the natural thing to do when I could no longer talk and be with her. She always loved my poetry and said that I was "the most romantic man". Naturally I wanted to go on doing that which satisfied her deeply and also satisfy my creative need to write.

I believe that I was emotionally unstable during the eight month period that I wrote this collection of poems. I spent many hours thinking of no one else but her. My work and home life suffered tremendously because I felt driven to communicate my feelings for her in poetic form. I admit that I ignored my family's needs at times and even my own health by not eating and sleeping properly. I loved Marilyn so deeply that nothing else seemed to matter. I kept wanting her to call and satisfy the special place deep within me that no one else could find. As the days went on without her voice, I began to get depressed. Writing was a suitable vent for purging my emotions that, I believe, kept me from losing my sanity. I still love her very deeply today, but I manage my feelings and emotions by channeling them into productive thinking. I will, no doubt, write about her in the future as I can never stop feeling her presence in my life. She is part of who I am now, sane or not.

The first poem in this collection, "As I Sleep", is a recollection of two dreams that I had months before I met Marilyn. At the time, I did not give much thought to these dreams as I frequently have very lucid and creative dreams that appear not to be related to any experience that I've had. After meeting, loving and losing Marilyn, I recalled these dreams as being significant. The woman in my dreams was Marilyn and the dreams were visions of her coming into my life. In the dreams, she never spoke to me verbally, rather I could feel what she was saying. I remember being excited and very happy in her presence but she wouldn't stay for long. She would fade away as my heart would yearn and plead, "come back, please, tell me more, please". It is interesting to me. In life, Marilyn came to me for a brief time and filled me with such excitement and joy only to fade away as I pleaded, wanting more.

During the time Marilyn and I were together, I never once thought of these dreams. Weeks after we parted, the memory of these dreams came back to me. I immediately knew it was her that I had dreamt of. I don't know for sure what dates I had the two dreams, and this poem was actually written in the fourth week of May 2000 shortly after we broke up. I picked September 27, 1999 as the date of the poem because it was close to the two dates of the dreams and it is also her birthday. My hope is that the significance of the two dreams is that she will return to my life a second time as she did in my dreams. I am torn, however, by the thought of losing her a second time. If it is to be, then the joy of having her a second time would be worth the pain of losing her again. I love her that much.

"As I Sleep"

As I sleep, she comes in flowing lace,
   In auburn glow and spirit free,
   Her eyes of emerald bath me
With love that is upon her face.
She has no name, yet I know her well.
   Calming and beautiful, near yet far.
   Within my dreams her images are
A vision of love as she foretells.
She does not speak, yet I hear her voice,
   Soothing my heart in passionate waves.
   In my essence, her message is deep.
Listen I must, for I have no choice.
   On an unknown shore, my life she saves,
   And kisses tomorrow awake, as I sleep.

"Steed" was written late during the night of the day of our first kiss. The kiss was very brief and was initiated by me. Marilyn walked me to the far end of the hallway on the floor that we worked on at the end of the day. I told her twice that week that I really wanted to put my arms around her and so she was giving me the opportunity. As we were about to part for the weekend, she reached for me and put her arms around me. We hugged briefly in a full body contact that felt so wonderful. I could feel her heart thumping against my chest. Her pelvis pressed firmly to mine as though she was saying "take me". As we pulled away from the hug, I looked into her eyes and was drawn to her sweet lips for the first time. Her lips were so soft and her tongue moved soft and slowly against mine. At that moment, I knew that I was going to love her and that life would never be the same.

We parted for the weekend with looks of disbelief. We were both surprised and very pleased by the kiss. My drive home was totally consumed by the thought of her and that kiss. This intense thinking carried over into the night as I found that I could not sleep. At or about three a.m., I began to write this poem. I was finished in about twenty minutes. After completing it, I got the idea that I would put a copy of it in an envelope and tape to the underside of her keyboard at work for a Monday morning surprise. I then sent an e-mail to her computer with instructions on where to find her surprise. The steamy nature of the poem stirred her so deeply inside, that she was not able to concentrate on her work. So we stole away to a quiet place at work to share our arms, eyes and lips.

"Steed"

Saddle me up at sunrise,
And take me out for a ride,
Of hot lusty multiple miles,
With a slow and easy glide.

Ride me slow and easy first,
And listen to your steed,
Breathe his lusty satisfaction
With the way your saddle feels.

Spank me with your reins,
And pace me for the distance.
Feel the connection strong between us,
And it's pulsing rubbing resistance.

Push me past my comfort speed,
And ride me till the morn is sunny.
Then turn me back towards we came,
As we mix our milk and honey.

Slow the gait and stroke my neck
With your reassuring hands.
Then race me home in a furious finish,
Sapping this steed of a man.

"Ocean Of Thee" is an Italian Sonnet that I began to write two weeks before Marilyn and I broke up. She was aware that I was writing this poem for her and was so excited about it. She said that no one had ever written poetry for her before and that she really loved the idea that I was inspired by her to write something special. After I completed the first two stanzas, I called her on the phone at work and read them to her. She said that my words were so wonderful and that she just loved the way that I thought. She said that I was just a naturally romantic man and "I just love you, love you, love you". She frequently expressed her love for me this way and it pleased me so much because I interpreted it to mean that saying it once was not enough to express what she really felt for me.

I worked on this poem slowly because I wanted it to be perfect. I told her that I wanted it to be the best and most beautiful poem that I had ever written because it was inspired by the most beautiful woman that I had ever known. I was so saddened by not having it finished before we broke up. I did tell her, however, that I would not let this work lay incomplete. I promised her that I would complete it so that one day she would be able to read it. I did not know how or when I would get it to her, but knew that I would. I did not work on it for many weeks after we broke up but when I did, I developed this deep desire to write poetry to and about her forever. This poem was the first of the fifty-three that followed in a quest to satisfy my need to express my deepest thoughts and feelings for the woman that still inspires me today as no one ever has.

"Ocean Of Thee"

My ship I sail in the loving ocean of thee.
   It lingers upon swells and gentle rolls,
    Touching the essence of an emerald soul.
In leagues and breadth it consumes me.
Pristine sunrise and set of thee I've seen.
   I've felt your gentle loving breeze
    Fill the sails of my soul and set my spirit free.
I've bask in your love aglow so pure and clean.
Upon horizons yore, my darkened past I've laid.
    The fleeting yesteryears
fade in peaceful grace
   While sailing thy ocean to
heaven's future shore.
Days are filled with waves of memories made.
   As your breeze whispers love upon my face,
   I commend my ship to thee forevermore.

I believe the first line of "I Wonder" was inspired by a conversation that Marilyn and I had about thunderstorms and lightening. I told her how much I loved snuggling in bed on stormy nights and watching the lightening flash against the bedroom walls. We talked about spooning all night with my hand holding her breast. She said that she really liked that. A few days later, while at a book store, she bought me a bookmark with a night storm scene with many lightning flashes. I still use that book mark today and think of her when I read.

Marilyn and I parted on May 10. The shock and pain of losing her left me floundering for nearly a month. During this time I did not write at all. I could not think rationally for extended periods of time. My creative abilities were at rock bottom and all I could do was manage the memories and pain. On June 2, I wondered if she was having similar difficulties. Many questions went through my mind as to how she might be coping with our break up. At that moment, my creative nature awakened. "I Wonder" seemed to be a gift from my sub-conscience mind to my conscience mind. I was merely a vehicle through which this work was expressed. I penned the first draft of this poem in ten minutes and made changes over the next hour. After finishing it, I marveled at what it made me feel. I languished in this poem for over a week wondering about her state of mind. I wanted desperately to share this poem with her though this was not possible. I had promised not to contact her so as to allow her time and space to put her life in order. But the power of this poem is yet unwavering. I still wonder about what she is thinking. I wonder if she can feel me thinking about her. I wonder if she misses me as much as I miss her.

"I Wonder"

If you think of me not, during storms at night,
    My name you whisper in moments of solitude?
    In happy thoughts, my spirit do you include
To bath upon your heart my lustrous light?
If our song yet resonates in your heart,
    Its lyrics paint a visage of our embrace?
    If you mourn your hands not holding my face
Or grieve a day without me in its start?
If you yearn "I love you" in baritone silk?
    If your fingers ache to reach for me
    As you muse in the morrow to see my face?
If the pain pierces your soul as strength doth wilt
    And temp our fate again,
for loving sake of "we"?
    If you wonder if "we" will endure
this time and space?

In retrospect, two months seem more like two years. "A Moment In Time" is about the seeming distortion in time. Marilyn and I spent so much time together talking on so many subjects, that is seems as if we have known each other for years. We talked in detail about our early lives. We discussed our deepest fears, our darkest mistakes, our early ambitions and our troubled marriages. Our conversations were about trying to help and heal each other by way of objectivity. One would listen while the other talked, then we would sooth with compassionate discussions, which served to draw us nearer to each other. Falling in love was so natural for us because we both knew how to care for the other's needs and pain. We allowed ourselves to fantasize about how wonderful life together would be if we were married. We spoke love with our eyes, touch, smiles and thoughts.

The two months that we spent together changed our lives at the fundamental level. We both learned important things about ourselves, our self-esteem, our self-worth and most importantly, the capacity of our hearts to self-love and be loved. There was a lifetime of loving and learning for us to explore but alas, the journey had to end. Though our time was brief, she has become a part of me for all of time to come. In this way, all of time is so compressed into a single word. That word is love. I shall love Marilyn for as long as my spirit and time exists.

"A Moment in Time"

In an instant, a moment in time,
Our worlds stopped spinning.
Two loving hearts became one,
And planned a new beginning.

So much of ourselves we shared,
In this short pulse of time,
So many dreams did blossom,
So many stars did shine.

In this moment, our spirts touched,
Exchanging and changing forever,
The way we look at life and love,
One without the other never.

Too short it was, a moment in time,
Not lasting the whole day long.
Our cup not nearly floweth over,
Before our moment gone.

By the time I began to write "Prison", I was in a confusing state of mixed emotions. I found that sadness and anger did not mix well. I was sure we had made the wrong decision about the paths our lives would take and my frustration was great because I wanted to tell her this. Only my promise not to contact her kept me from doing so. My deepest desire was for her to be happy. I did not want to risk making her unhappy by breaking my promise to her. Even today I must remind myself that my word to her has to mean something if ever there will be a chance for us in the future.

Five days after I wrote "Prison", I wrote "Elegy In Purgatory" which also is a dark poem lamenting my destitute state of mind. "Prison" and "Elegy" are in my mind, a set, conveying the same dark message. "Elegy" is one of my favorites in the collection however because it begins in a deep, dark, setting and ends with a faintly lit declaration of hope. My spirit was wounded but the hope of future love and happiness sustained me until I could regain my strength. "Elegy" represents a turning point, both for me and the style and composition of the poems that would follow. I am beginning, at this point, to accept that I am not going to hear her voice or look deep into her eyes for some time to come. I found that recalling specific moments that we shared filled me with her warmth and reminded me that the beauty of her love still lives in me. I realized that if she lived in me, I could visit her spirit anytime and as often I liked. In this way, she sustained me through what would be some very difficult months ahead.

"Prison"

In what prison have we bound our love
That light not shown for promise to others?
It threatens forever the very life it smothers,
And rends us for righteous sake of.

Within these walls, our quietus bought.
Prior rites wrest us this way,
To seal the circle "we" for some future day.
This time is what life has wrought.

How vast this prison, its midst we find our lot?
Flung here we by guilt or benevolent cause?
We did fail to observe nuptial laws.
In our days of bliss, our others we forgot.

In this prison, we sit, we cry, we ache,
Anguishing this fate, as bliss again we'll make.

"Ode To M" and "M And I", like "Prison" and "Elegy In Purgatory", are a set. But there is where the similarities end. At this point in time, I had begun to focus on the love for Marilyn that still burned in my heart rather than lamenting the pain of our loss. I am beginning to understand how channeling my thoughts and emotions into these beautiful poetic works serves me and hopefully one day "us". I found that writing these two poems was much easier and much more satisfying. Further evidence of the ease and joy that I was finding in writing to Marilyn can be seen by looking at the numbers of poems I was writing each month. "Ode To M" was the first of nine poems that I wrote in July. In August there were ten and in September there were fifteen. During this time period, I am writing every day whenever the inspiration hits me. I frequently would be in the middle of some extremely complicated project at work that required me to focus so sharply that I would not be aware of what was going on around me. Then I would get these beautiful thoughts and inspirations. I would always yield to these times and write what I felt. They were like a narcotic that I couldn't say no to. Marilyn would and always will come first.

"Ode" is a reflection back to the two dreams I had that inspired the poem "As I Sleep". It seemed appropriate to go back to the beginning with this fresh outlook and work my way through our romance expressing the full range of emotions that I felt. "M And I" was a soft reflection on the gentle nature of our relationship. Both of these poems end with a note of optimism about the future return of our love.

"Ode To M"

She came as foretold into my life
And breathed in me the love
Which promised to end all strife.
She came to me from above.

With spirit as that of an angel,
Her voice yet resonates in my heart.
The stars in her eyes did spangle,
The night of my life and lit the dark.

Into my tapestry she wove her magic,
Breathing hope for future joy.
Her loss is all day tragic.
Unto God, her return I implore.

She saved my essence from the cold abyss.
And sealed our future with a loving kiss.

"M And I"

In the space of our moment,
Our hearts entwine did we,
To share our loving natures,
For all the world to see.

We wrote some loving messages,
Among the clouds in the sky,
And promised each the future,
Did my loving M and I.

Hands we held, miles we walked,
The road to forever did we,
We witnessed for each other,
What loving bliss could be.

Now we wait to find,
What in the morrow lie.
We bide our time apart today,
My loving M and I.

"Elegy in Purgatory"

What tomb by name has love been cast,
Oh walls of dank and gray?
Where light not shed and pain doth last,
And night envelops the day.

Foreboding pitch was not perceived,
By precept this burden wrought.
For sake of others, love is cleaved,
Time entombed angst of thought.

Suffering ennui and spirit dark,
Hope keeps love alive.
Oh labyrinth tomb from whence I hark,
My spirit lives as love survives.

Love doth cling to a sunrise sweet,
When Purgatory's penitence is but complete.

"Interlude" was born of a single abstract thought while sitting on the deck in my yard. I was deep in thought as I looked to the west, watching the sun set. Because Marilyn lives in a small rural town northwest of where I live, I sit and face that direction in the evenings and think of her sitting next to me with the late evening sun on her hair and face. I used to tell her how beautiful she was with the sun on her face. I often wonder if she is watching the same sunset while thinking of me.

On that day, I became aware of my breathing for some reason. At that moment, the thought for this poem was born. The thought was that I loved her so much that I even thought of her in those spaces between the important events in our lives, such as the small amount of time between each breath. Never have I contemplated the time between breaths before, but since our breakup, I view everything differently.

I've developed a love, hate relationship with time. Time is what we both need to heal our hearts. But there is a finite amount of time in our lives and it is ticking away while we are apart. I feel it in my core that we will one day be together again and this interlude in our love will be over. The temptation is to wish this remaining time away but in-so-doing, hasten our final days of our life. And so I am left to watch the sun pacing the day away as I consider the ticks of time and the interludes between.

"Interlude"

What thoughts give we
To eddies between events?
The irretractable ticking
To which no homage lent.

Between our glances,
Your wispy touch.
Between the kisses
We love so much.

Between our breaths,
Our hearts do sing,
Those future days where
There's no between.

Those future days do preclude,
A likened state of this interlude.

"I'll Wait For You" is about my resolve to never surrender my undying love for Marilyn. I realized there was some lingering feelings of anger about the decision we made. These feelings were working on my will not to give up and move on. I made a resolute decision to never let this happen. She is such a part of me that I could never not love her. Some days I struggled with my emotional and rational sides. They were fighting inside of me for control. At times, I felt like a mediator of two unruly children who would not behave. This poem is about tough love. It is about serving notice to my inner tormentors that no matter how long this battle raged, I would never allow my love for Marilyn to die.

I am beginning to question the state of my sanity at this time. But through it all, what I felt in my heart and soul never wavered. I told myself that if I were going to lose my sanity, I would simply be crazy in love with her and that I really didn't particularly care which side of my mind rested on. Loving her is akin to loving me. Marilyn improved my self-image and my self-love as she became a part of me. Allowing her love to die in me would be allowing a part of me to die. That, I can never do. I am so in love with her and the "me" that she helped to make, that I don't ever want to change.

I really do intend to wait for her for however long it takes. If that is into eternity, then so be it.

"I'll Wait For You"

I'll wait for you Darling,
Until day and night are one,
Until the birds fail to sing,
Until the moon joins the sun.

I'll not let one day go by,
Without savory thoughts of your kiss,
Without seeing your loving smile,
Without needing the arms I so miss.

I'll wait through the dark and hurt,
Through each moment of despair.
I'll wait to the end of this world,
Until the sea is turned to air.

I'll wait until the heavens turn cold,
To join our love and make us whole.

During the time period when I wrote "Yonder Light", I was writing every day. I was getting such a flood of beautifully poetic thoughts. At times, it was a little frustrating because I would get these thoughts while I was very busy with something important and time demanding. I would always yield to these thoughts and write them down. I imagined they were beautiful thoughts sent to me somehow by Marilyn. And, as I have stated, I would never say no to her.

I remember thinking how overwhelmed she would probably be by the number of poems in this work. I had only mentioned one sonnet to her before we broke up. Marilyn is quick to tears when something touches her deeply. I really like that about her. She has no fear of displaying her emotions and showing her vulnerable side. Holding her during those times satisfied a place deep within me. It is the place where my manhood is centered. I need to be the rock that she leans on when she is at her weakest. I suspect that many of these poems will touch her to tears. The shear number of poems will no doubt cause her a touching moment. I want to be there to hold her in my arms at that moment.

"Yonder Light" is a symbolic poem about our love. The light in the poem is the flame of our love and I am needing many answers about the state of our true feelings and plans for each other. I answered the question of where my heart was by asking the flame to consume me altogether by adding my name to the list of conquered in love. What's missing in this poem are her answers to all of the questions that it asks.

"Yonder Light"

What yonder light I see?
Is it illusion or is it we?
Does our candle yet heat,
Perchance again our hands to meet?

What past fuels its glow?
What does it want me to know?
Provocative dancer, it beckons me.
Is our joining meant to be?

My heart warms from far away,
Conjuring images of yesterday.
Quietly it speaks of future time,
When distance then is all behind.

Yonder light, oh beautiful flame,
Consume my soul and take my name.

I love delicate symbolism in my writing. "Our Flower" fits this genre so well. Few things in life are more delicate than a flower. I perceive Marilyn's nature to be that of a sweet, fragrant and beautiful flower. It was quite natural for me to think of our love in this way. Beautiful flowers have a softening effect on me and I always yield to the feelings they evoke. I really love growing flowers as they appeal very strongly to three of the five senses.

I once told Marilyn that we were growing our love like a beautiful flower. Everything in our relationship had a proper time in that growth and that we should tend to the growth of our relationship with the same kind of loving care. One day, very early in our relationship, Marilyn brought a potted ivy to work for her desk. She said it was a special plant that she wanted to watch grow to see how beautiful it would get. I took her words to be symbolic of her wanting to watch our love grow into a beautiful flower. When she and I parted, she left the plant in my care. It's like a child from our union that reminds me of her as I love and nurture it.

"Our Flower" is about the love that she and I grew from the seeds of our friendship in the fertile soil of truth and trust. We nurtured our love daily and cared for it so well. Our flower yet blooms even though we are apart and cannot tend it together as we once did. The darkest day cannot darken the beautiful glow of our love. The love that we share yearns our hands and eyes to tend it again.

"Our Flower"

From the seeds of our love,
Grew a beautiful flower.
Fragrantly blooming it does,
Even in this darkened hour.

Upon its face, light yet shines.
Thriving in fertile thoughts,
Of days we sipped our savory wine,
It waits again this way we walk.

Our flower yearns our loving hands,
To tend its growth in love.
When hearts are bound by golden bands,
And Blessed by God above.

Its fragrant bouquet fills the air,
And seeks again our eyes we share.

Marilyn had the most wonderful smile. You got the feeling that she was enjoying giving you that something special there was in her eyes when she smiled. Many times I found myself mesmerized, not hearing a word she was saying. I'm not sure she fully understood the effect her smile had on me. I told her many times how much I loved it, but we were usually lost in each other's arms kissing soulfully deep when I did. I would look into her passionate eyes as she gave me that smile. At that moment, she had me. I was so captivated, that she could have taken advantage of me if she so desired and it would have been perfectly fine with me. Her smile also had a lingering after effect somewhat like the lasting after effect of incredibly great sex. I always had this great feeling and strong memory of her smile after she left the room. I once told her that every time she kissed me that I stayed kissed for a long time afterwards. I know that it was because of that smile and look in her eyes.

Making her laugh and smile became one of my favorite pass times. I know that made her feel good enough to share her smile with me. I now admit that my motives were selfish.

"When She Smiles" was written late at night when the city was dark and quiet. It is then that I miss her most. When the beneficial background noise of day to day life has abated and I am left alone with my thoughts and memories of our love, her smile is always first to greet me with the warmth which says "I just love you so very much Luster".

"When She Smiles"

When she smiles, I am at peace,
And the world seems to go away.
I cast my spirit in depths of she,
To return some other day.

When she smiles, my heart sings,
A song with lyrics sweet.
Each note a heavenly ring,
Embracing our love complete.

When she smiles, I'm in a place,
Where only she has presence.
Total joy envelops my face,
And lovingly bathes my essence.

When she smiles, I am improved,
As into my heart, heaven moves.

When I wrote "Silly We", I was in a very silly mood. I used to get silly with Marilyn once in a while because she brought out the little boy in me. She thought it was cute but I got the impression that she had a short limit with this kind of behavior. I never once saw her acting silly and so I think it was not a part of her basic nature. This is not to say that she was too serious and lacking the ability to have fun. Quite the opposite was true. Fun was very important to her, especially when it came to playing with me. Fun for her was more adult like and, oh my, did she know how to have fun. Often, when we had lunch with our co-workers, we would position ourselves so that we could play under the table while we ate. No one ever know how much we were enjoying our lunch. Sometimes she would take off her shoe and put her foot in my lap and massage me to the point of excitement. Marilyn had very talented toes that knew exactly how to touch and stroke. Her brand of play could never be labeled silly but it sure was fun.

I believe that I wanted her to see the little boy in me because at forty-nine, I was five years older than she. Subconsciously I believed I was concerned with her thinking maybe I was a little too old to be fun. I knew that I wasn't but I needed her to know that. I also wanted her to see the multi-dimensional aspect of my personality. I can be serious, silly, sensuous, sedate, sexy and very seductive. I don't believe that I ever bored or disappointed her.

Although "Silly We" was written while in one of my silly moods and my intent was to write a silly little poem, it didn't turn out that way. During the two days that followed, I revised it, making changes that made it less and less silly. I was no longer in a silly mood and found it impossible to be silly about losing the love of my life. It endures as one of my favorites in the collection.

"Silly We"

What a silly we,
Our heads thick with sleep.
We should have seen this coming,
When hearts we plunged so deep.

Mercy, mercy oh pitiful we,
Did sacrifice our trusts.
We cause our others not to smile,
When look they do upon us.

Silly we, silly we,
To think we'd run away.
We'd give the past to the winds,
With hearts that laughed and played.

Silly we to think us this,
That started with a Friday kiss.

After my failed attempt at silly poetry, I became very serious with my poetry to Marilyn. I remember feeling guilty about the original idea and thought to myself that being silly at a time like this would not please her at all. The poem that followed, "If" was, in my mind, an apology for such a mental lapse. I tried to pack as many suppositions as I could into the fourteen line structure of this poem. I wanted to reassure her that my love was not a whimsical and fleeting feeling characterized by childishness.

I chose the word "if" as the title for this work, because of its association with the vastness of possibilities. I wanted her to know that no matter what conditions existed in the natural world, they would not dampen my deep and abiding love for her. The most unlikely of possible conditions would not change the way that I felt. My love for her was, and still is, beyond the realm of the physical world and therefore unaffected by the events therein. It transcends time and space. If only I could tell her this.

The suppositions put forth in this poem are extreme. If they ever existed, the world would be in dire condition. Removing the world "if" from the beginning of each line results in a declarative statement which captures the essence of my world since we parted. The sun fails to rise, the birds refuse to sing, the skies are all with clouds of gray, but this doesn't mean a thing. As long as there is hope and eternity, I'll love her and wait for our rejoining.

"If"

If the sun failed to rise,
If the birds refuse to sing,
If the sky were all with clouds of gray,
It wouldn't mean a thing.

If the hands of time took rest,
If the sea didn't rush to shore,
If our eyes could never meet again,
I'd have nothing to live for.

If the world itself stopped turning,
If the night replaced the day,
If the sounds of life went silent,
I'd love you anyway.

If I have to wait for eternity,
Then wait I shall for we.

The next two months would be a very intense period of writing for me. I wrote whenever the inspiration hit me, no matter where I was or what I was doing. I seemed to have so much to say and so little time to say it. I knew that Marilyn's birthday was nearing and I wanted somehow to get this body of poetry finished and to her as a gift. Of course, when I wrote, "I Miss You", I was nowhere near being finished. I convinced myself that I could have all fifty-four poems finished by her birthday on September twenty-seventh. And so I poured myself into this effort like never before. For the next two months, I averaged a complete poem every two days. I seemed to thrive on the pressure of trying to meet this personal deadline that I had set for myself. It was during this time period that my work and home life suffered most.

Sometimes I would get an idea for a poem and all I would have would be a title or a few lines. I would stop and make notes and come back to it later. I even kept a note pad on the stand next to my bed so that if I had a dream as an inspiration, I could make notes and avoid the risk of not remembering in the morning.

My approach to writing "I Miss You" was to first make a list of all of the things about Marilyn that I missed. The list was so long that I couldn't possibly get it all into the short style of the poems in this collection. I decided to narrow my list by selecting the things about her that I most liked and missed. This was still a difficult task. In fact, it was easier writing the poem than it was making those selections.

"I Miss You"

I miss you my love,
In ways you may never know.
I miss you on my mountaintops,
And from my valleys low.

I miss the loving look in your eyes,
You gave me when we'd kiss.
I miss that short gasping breath,
When your passion filled with bliss.

I miss your loving voice,
When you'd call me sweetly, Hun.
I miss the way we laughed together,
And always had such fun.

I miss the way you stroked my arms,
With your tender loving hands,
And made me feel that in this world,
I was the only man.

I miss the anticipation,
Of seeing you at the top of my day.
But I cannot miss the hurt that's left,
From the day you went away.

For many weeks, I thought of Marilyn so intensely that I just knew that she could feel my thoughts. I knew she was feeling the pain in my heart and soul. In my mind's eye, I could see sadness on her face when she was alone with her memories. I ached for her because I didn't want her to be sad. I also ached because I needed her with me to fill up my senses. But, her sadness was an indication that she still loved me and missed me as much as I missed her.

I suppose that it was actually easier to believe and accept her being sad and lonely than it would have been for me to know that she did not miss or think of me at all. That pain would have been worse because it would have meant I was alone in love. I know of no colder environ that that. The pain of not having her in my life became more bearable after I realized that there was a condition that was more painful than the one that we were suffering.

With this thought in mind, I wrote "Be Still" as a plea for her to feel the pain in my heart so that she would know that she was not alone in love. I told Marilyn in our last conversation that she would never be alone in the world and that no matter how bad things got, she always has a friend. I told her that she could call me anytime, anywhere and I'd be there for her. My greatest desire is for her to be happy in life no matter whom with. This poem is a prayerful reminder to her that I am waiting out there to fulfill her life and make us both happy again. If the choice that we made does not work out, we'll always have each other.

"Be Still"

Be still my love and close your eyes,
Listen to my broken heart sing.
A mournful song of feeble ring.
In darkened hue anguished it lies.

Be still my Sweet and see the pain,
Upon my tear stained cheeks.
For I've not lived these many weeks,
When we, from each other, refrained.

Be still my M and hear my voice,
Calling you from afar,
To say that our situations are,
The result of a really bad choice.

Be still my Sweet, know this fact,
I really do need and want you back.

Marilyn and I used the word "but" in our conversations as a comic-relief from the serious reality of our situation. We used it as a conjunction between our fantasies and our realities, usually evoking a laugh or a smile. We loved each other deeply and knew in our hearts and souls that we were so right for each other. I wonder how life could have been so cruel as to bring us together in this situation where neither of us was free to have the other completely.

I liked the fact that she could make me laugh and smile as I would her. Our fantasies were much more fun because our realities were so painful. Finding something to laugh and smile about drew us closer to each other. We learned to depend on each other for that "good feeling fix" every day because our realities hurt.

I wrote "But I Do" during my lunch hour at work. It is one of my favorites in the collection. It is the only poem in the collection that I did not edit after writing. I read this poem many times in the weeks after writing it in an attempt to find a way to squeeze more feeling into it. But the more I read it, the more I was sure it was perfect just the way it was. I knew that I was torturing myself by not letting go of her and going on with what was left of the life that I knew. My love for Marilyn was so strong that I couldn't and didn't want to let go. My rational mind was saying that this kind of thinking was not good for me. But my heart was saying it would not be denied the right to feel what was, and still is, the purest and deepest love that I have ever known. I know that I'm not supposed to love Marilyn, but I do. And I will let nothing change that.

"But" I Do

I'm not supposed to think of us,
And the love that we once knew.
I'm not supposed to miss your smiles,
In the top of my day, "but" I do.

I'm not supposed to long for the arms,
That held me so close to you.
I'm not supposed to need your kiss,
On my face and lips, "but" I do.

I'm not supposed to think of us,
Alone in a love-lock for two.
I'm not supposed to need your touch,
As I lay down to sleep, "but" I do.

I'm not supposed to dream of the day,
When our hearts are bound as glue.
I'm not supposed to love you, Dear,
In the depths of my soul, "but" I do.

Einstein once said "to know is nothing, but to imagine is everything". As a young man, I took this quote to heart. I realized at an early age that there was something special about the ability to conjure up ideas from nothing more than an inspiration. Through many years of practice, I have developed this ability as a part of my basic nature. In fact, I think it is the element of me that I derive the most pleasure from. Creating something from your own thoughts is much like giving birth. All of my projects are like children to me. I conceive, birth and nurture and cherish them as one would a child.

Marilyn and I frequently fantasize about what life would be like if we could have each other totally. The conversations were full of wonder and passion. We both had very vivid imaginations and loved to share our thoughts. She once told me that if we were married, we would get nothing done because we wouldn't be able to break away from each other's arms. I imagined this to be a true statement. Holding her was heavenly. She seemed to nestle her body to me in a way which seemed to match all of my contours. The visual image of what she would look like if this was so is kind of squirrely, but that's what it felt like. She was a perfect fit.

There is some evidence in the scientific community that supports the idea of influencing positive outcomes based on strong positive mental imagery. With this thought in mind, I wrote "Imagine". It is unique because it takes imagination to write poetry and this poem is about imaginings. This poem speaks of total bliss from sun up to sun down, which is what we both wanted our life together to be. Maybe if we both imagine very intensely, the words of this poem will come to fruition.

"Imagine"

Imagine us awakening to we,
In a tender and sensuous way.
Imagine life with sun on your face,
Each and every day.

Imagine spending the entire day,
With me and only me.
Discussing what is dear to us,
While sipping our foo-foo tea.

Imagine life, troubled free,
In perfect harmony walked.
Seeing the world through loving eyes,
While sharing our every thought.

Imagine walking hand in hand,
Lingering on love's long beach,
While kissing slow and tenderly,
In depths, our souls we'd reach.

Imagine the sun, setting low,
On our paradise in bliss,
Ending each wonderfully perfect day,
With a loving sleepy kiss.

When I fell in love with Marilyn, life exploded with fresh new colors and emotions. The air was suddenly filled with the fragrant aroma of new flowers. Old thoughts and ideas were replaced with new budding beauty. Aspiration and anticipation spring from the fertile ideas we shared as life was awash with the most beautiful promise I had ever experienced. The tears that we shed together were like a loving spring rain that soothed the dry, parched landscape of our lives. They brought old pains to the surface to be cleansed away and provided sustenance for the growth of our new love.

Our love truly was like a spectacular spring that coincidentally, occurred during the spring of the year. Our days were bright and sunny. The birds sang newly written, beautiful songs just for us. Every sunrise held promise and every sunset held hope for the next day to come. Every moment together was precious and every moment apart was filled with the anticipation of rejoining our eyes, arms and lips. Deeper and deeper we fell with no indication that we would find a limit. But one day in May we did. That limit was our realities. On that day we found a pain greater than any before.

"Falling In Love" begs the question as to why the fall of love can't go on forever. I truly believe that had Marilyn and I been free to have each other completely, we would have fallen in our love for the rest of our life together. Heaven on earth would have been found and every day would have been love's spectacular spring.

"Falling In Love"

Being in love is a wondrous thing,
Not nearly so much as the fall.
The fall is love's spectacular spring,
Its' blossom consumes you all.

Falling in love is full of surprise,
And wonderment to behold.
Passion fills the look in your eyes,
For want of things untold.

Exploring the realm of what will be,
As fantasies flow between,
Sharing your very souls with each,
In free fall lover's dreams.

Deeper and deeper, the abyss of bliss,
This beautiful story unfolds,
Where hearts and lips forever kiss,
In loving arms you hold.

Why can't the fall go on forever,
With nothing to cause its break?
Where falling in love becomes life itself,
And heaven on earth it makes.

After finishing "Falling In Love", I went into a mini-depression that lasted about a week. During that time, I felt sorry for myself and did not manage my pain very well. On more than one occasion, I picked up the phone and dialed Marilyn's number only to hang up before it started to ring.

It was an extremely, long, hot and dry summer in Texas. The sun baked every ounce of moisture out of the landscape rendering a scored effect where ever you looked. I have no doubt that this weather condition contributed in some way to this state of depression that I found myself in. It occurred to me that this was what a summer in hell must have looked and felt like. It certainly was the exact opposite of what the spring of the year had been for Marilyn and I. Then, everything was lush, green and moist with abundant splashes of colorful flowers. Being in love heightened our senses to the beauty of everything around us.

The summer of 2000 was indeed like hell for me. The extreme heat somehow seemed appropriate to the loss we had experienced. But as in any bad situation, I try to find something good to hinge my optimism on. What I found was that the miserable hell of losing Marilyn had tempered my resolve much in the same way a piece of metal is hardened by heat treating. The extreme hell tested my metal to determine just how strong my love for her was. I came out of this mini-depression with the inspiration for "Hell's Summer" and a new found certainty that no matter how bad things got, I could survive until she and I could be together again. I had survived hell's summer and in the process, was tempered to a new level of strength and resolve.

"Hell's Summer"

Out of the ashes this pit,
From whence my spirit plummet,
Has risen a deeper love,
Tempered by hell's summer.

These days have heavily tolled,
He that I used to be,
Rendering straight the face,
Where smiles the world would see.

Within this spirit, charred and black,
No luster shown from these eyes.
Nothing left of this soul but hope,
And need for you by my side.

Hell's summer allowed me to see,
The depth of my love for you,
Convicting resolve to one day align,
These hearts that now beat as two.

Hell's summer has strengthened me,
In ways I couldn't have known,
And left me sure as never before,
That your heart is my true home.

"Midnight Train" is a sensuously naughty poem inspired by a conversation that Marilyn and I had about riding in a train across country. She had worked for the railroad earlier in her life and must have loved it very much. She had a sparkle in her eyes when she talked about it. I had never ridden across country on a train and so we fantasized about us traveling together this way. Marilyn did most of the talking in this conversation as I was just along for the ride. What a wonderful ride it was that she took me on.

Most of the conversation was centered around having a sleeper car and the love sessions we would have each night and day while on our trip. At some point in our conversation, I remember feeling a sensation of rocking from side to side as she talked about making love to the rhythm of the train's movement. She talked about making love slow and easy all night, tenderly holding each other and looking deep into our eyes as we satisfied each other over and over. We'd fall asleep from exhaustion only to be awakened by stirring passions for another lengthy session of bliss. She really knew how to make me burn with desire for her. Marilyn was an incredibly gifted and sensuous woman.

I had a difficult time trying to finish this poem because I wanted it to go on and on like the love sessions she described. I wanted this poem to capture the essence of that conversation in a way that would stir the reader with imagination and lust. I succeeded in stirring myself while writing this poem. But I have the vivid memories of holding Marilyn in my arms and being whisked to a place far away, a place that I desperately want to return to. That place is sensuously naughty and her arms are waiting there to pull me into her body and become one again.

"Midnight Train"

On the steel hard rail,
In the cool darkened air,
The midnight train rolls,
Into a sensuous lair.

Without rhythmic faults,
It rocks the rail, it sways.
It's throaty engine pulsing,
Fantasies of adventurous ways.

The gentle roll pleasure the ride,
Merging our love and souls,
Pulsing vibes all through us,
Dizzying thoughts, trembling toes.

Through each small town,
We rock with its every roll.
One with its locomotion,
As our love's blossom unfolds.

We ride the rail throughout the night,
With nary a stop for air.
Our furnace full with passion fire,
And our destination near.

As we greet the dawning sun,
The midnight train and we,
The steam hot whistle blows,
It's pleasure song so sweet.

I love the use of a metaphor in my writing. It allows for the cross utilization of concepts and feelings that are difficult to express otherwise. In the poem "A River Between Us", I used the massive energy of a river to describe the love that flows between Marilyn and I. I seem to be prone to the use of metaphor and simile because of the non-equivalency limitation of the English language. The love that she and I share does not literally make a sound, but in my perception it roars like a mighty river flowing incessantly towards its destination.

Our river's waters are calm at the surface because our relationship was calm and gentle. But under the surface was such a dynamic passion that we found our attraction irresistible. In a conversation early in our relationship, she admitted to me that she was struggling with the morality of our relationship. I told her that I too was having the same problem and that maybe we should not take this any further. She began to cry and it nearly broke my heart. At that moment I knew we had something special. I told her that she and I did not choose to have this over powering chemistry between us. She agreed and so we decided to ride the river to see where it would take us. It carried us to the deep and pure love that we both had inside of us to give that had been waiting for the other to come along to receive.

Though Marilyn and I are no longer together, our river of love yet flows and forever will. We are just not riding it together as before. I think we both can still feel the energy of our river and hear its mighty roar. It is a background sound that reminds us of what we had and could have again if the conditions were right and we chose to. I'm committed to letting our river take its course and hope that it leads us back to each other at some point in time.

"A River Between Us"

There flows a river between us,
Endless, deep and strong.
Towards the vast ocean we,
Flowing day and night long.

It's width, the days of two months,
But I know not of its depth
For it increases with time and love,
Not limited to life itself.

The river that flows between us,
Shall flow for time on end,
Giving life to hope and love,
And promise an eternal friend.

I'm drawn to the river between us,
By its irresistible force.
I lay down my soul upon it,
And let the river take its course.

Each night as I am about to go to sleep, I whisper Marilyn's name and tell her that I love her. My hope is that she somehow hears my voice across time and distance. My prayer each night is for us to dream about each other. I have wondered what it would be like if we could meet in our dreams each night and experience each other as we wished. How wonderful it would be to have a unified dream state where we both interacted together for the realities of our separate worlds. "Meet Me In My Dreams" is about such a concept.

When Marilyn and I were together, I did not dream of her. Since our relationship was founded on truth and trust, I told her that I had not dreamed of her. She was surprised and, I think, a little hurt. I told her she was my last thought before I went to sleep and my first thought when I woke up. She occupied most of my thoughts during my waking hours only being interrupted occasionally by work and family matters. During our relationship, I had an extremely difficult time sleeping. I would wake up with her on my mind every night between one and two A.M. and could not go back to sleep. Maybe that is why I didn't dream of her. I wasn't sleeping long enough each night to dream.

"Meet Me In My Dreams" is like a prayer that I think or whisper before I go to sleep at night. Her meeting me in my dreams would be second only to having her back in my life. Now that would be a dream come true.

"Meet Me In My Dreams"

Meet me in my dreams,
And look into my soul,
To find the well of love for you,
And beauty yet untold.

Meet me in my dreams,
And hold me close my Dear.
Push aside the pain we share,
And cast away our fear.

Meet me in my dreams,
And bring your tender lips.
The lips that well my passion stir,
That quiver my fingertips.

Meet me in my dreams,
And say you love me still.
Whisper Luster softly Sweet,
As need for each we fill.

Meet me in my dreams,
And help me plan a day.
The day when we come back to we,
And never go away.

It is my belief that when two people share their spirts, they are bound for all of time to be part of each other. The memories and emotions shared cannot be erased and therefore influences you in some way for the rest of your life. This is true for me with Marilyn. She has had such a positive influence in my life and still does today with every breath that I take.

We had a conversation about how empty and desperate our lives had been. We related to each other how the dark events in our pasts had served to make life, in general a rather unpleasant experience. Because we were so open with our deepest feelings, I told her something that I had never told another person. For many years, I consumed too much alcohol. Each night I would drink until it was time to go to bed. Before I dozed off to sleep, I would pray to God that he take me from this world while I was asleep. Life was so painful, I just didn't want to live anymore. I would never, ever commit suicide, but I did lose my will to live. I believe that is why I drank so much alcohol. When I told her this, she stroked my arm very gently and told me she didn't ever want me to feel that way again. She made me know that I was worthy of her love and that I had something special to live for.

Deep, open and honest conversations like this are the footsteps that we made in the sands of our shore. The memories are strong and true. They cannot be washed away by time. "Footsteps In The Sand" reminds me of every loving conversation we had and what real love and truth mean to me. Because of Marilyn, I no longer pray to God to take me while I sleep. Because of Marilyn, I love sunrise, sunset and all that happens between.

"Footsteps In The Sand"

My days I spend walking,
In our footsteps in the sand
Along the silent, empty shore,
Of Luster and Marilyn.

Each step, a memory cherished,
Tides of time can't wash away
They fill my senses so complete,
Consuming my entire day.

I look to sea for the ship of thee,
But it doesn't pass this land.
So I relive our memories there,
In our footsteps in the sand.

I pray you turn your ship about,
This way you sail again.
I pray, together we one day walk,
In our footsteps in the sand.

The sun sets low, on tears I shed,
Near the ocean of life called we,
Along the shore where our footsteps are,
That forever after shall be.

"Dance With Me" is not a poem about dancing. It was inspired by one of our conversations about dancing, but is actually about us spending the rest of our lives together in a happy, playful and passionate way. These terms best characterize our relationship.

We talked about dancing and how she wanted to learn but didn't get any support at home. I love to dance and told her that I wanted to teach her so that we could go dancing together. She smiled so big and pretty. I could see her thoughts as she looked deep into my eyes. "Finally, a man who is strong and sensitive enough to recognize and satisfy my needs as a woman". I told her that while dancing slowly with her all night, I would actually be making love to her mind. It's like extremely extremely erotic foreplay, but it's done in public on the dance floor. We would then go home and burn up the bed with the passion that we stirred in each other. Dancing together is something that we really wanted to do and never got the chance.

"Dance With Me" is about the merging of two spirits that dance forever after to the loving symphony of a happy life. It is about sharing every aspect of ourselves, about sharing every thought and every fear. It is about the joining of two hearts into one that beat to its own beautiful music. It is also about a deep hope that fate will one day, give us this dance for the rest of time. Our spirits will embrace forever in a loving dance and the music will never stop.

∞

"Dance With Me"

Dance with me like a school girl,
All giddy with fun and play.
Dance from yonder sunset light,
Into tomorrow's day.

Dance with me my love,
In surrealistic dreams.
Wisk my spirit to places,
Far from ordinary things.

Spin me dizzy with your love,
In surrealistic dreams.
Wisk my spirit to places,
Far from ordinary things.

Spin me dizzy with your love,
Then hold me closely Dear,
And slowly waltz my passion hot,
As we share our passion tears.

Feel my arms around you tight,
As we sync our every thought.
Taste the wine upon my lips,
To know what our love has wrought.

Dance with me my Marilyn,
For the rest of our beautiful life.
Dance with me in heart and soul,
The night you become my wife.

It was getting close to Marilyn's birthday by the time that I wrote "A Special Place Within". I had counted the days and number of poems left to write and knew that I would not be finished by September twenty-seventh. There were only twenty days left and twenty-seven poems to write. And so I changed my plan and moved the completion date to my birthday on the twenty-seventh of November so as to take the pressure off the quality of the poetry. After all, quality is far more important to Marilyn than quantity. She's a quality person. I did, however, continue to write at a fervent pace, primarily because the feelings were flowing so well. I wanted to capture every nuance of every thought before it was diluted by time. Bread is always best when right out of the oven.

September was the most prolific month of writing in my life. This did not surprise me given the inspiration I had. I wrote fifteen poems in September averaging almost one a day. The first was written on the fifth and the last two on the twenty-seventh. I felt so relaxed and really enjoyed the experience of writing during this time.

"A Special Place Within" is a poem about Marilyn's place in my heart and soul. She has become such a part of me that I literally can feel and hear her. It's as if we are connected somehow. All of her speech patterns, the way she walks, her laugh, even the touch of her hands so softly are a part of who I am now. I find that retreating to this wonderland within me is actually good for my spirit. It lifts me in a way that nothing else can. I believe the love that I have for her is growing in fertile soils of a special place within me and forever after will.

"A Special Place Within"

There is a place inside of me,
Reserved for only you.
I go there morning, noon and night,
To feel you love me too.

This place is warm and safe,
With light from your genuine love.
I bask and linger in your glow,
And play with your spirit dove.

This place is like an opiate,
As it controls my day.
I give my mostly time to it,
As I while my life away.

I'd rather have reality with you,
Though I know this thought is a sin.
So I retreat to you each day,
In a special place within.

In a very real way, Marilyn and I had committed our lives to each other. We had so many conversations about our future together and how wonderful life would be. Many times we discussed being married and talked of all of the things we would do and places we would go. We even talked of moving away from the United States to the UK, where the country side and people were so beautiful. She had visited there on vacation some years before we met and had fallen in love with it. She brought pictures of her trip there to work one day and guided me through her vacation while we had lunch. Afterwards, I felt as though I had been there with her. She talked so passionately and the vistas were so breathtakingly beautiful. I had never seen green hillsides so brilliantly alluring before. The pictures couldn't have been as beautiful as the actual countryside, yet they and her passionate words swept me away on a noontime journey as only she could do.

Marilyn knew where all of my buttons were and knew exactly how and when to push them. More importantly she knew that it was important to me to have those buttons pushed by her and she took such care in doing so. I know that she and I were made for each other. In all of my years, no one has felt so right for me.

The Poem "I Do's" is about the spoken and unspoken words our hearts and souls shared. I believe the beautiful words, thoughts and feelings we shared during our romance still live in us and wait patiently for us to return to the days we so passionately planned.

No matter how long or how far away from each other we are, our deep love binds us in a way that cannot be broken.

"I Do's"

Without so much as a whisper,
We've spoken two beautiful words.
We've seen our thoughts on the subject we,
We know what our hearts have heard.

We've listened to beautiful songs they sing,
With every love filled beat.
And felt the pulsing rhythm of love,
From heads down to our feet.

Our sundering chasm, now wide and deep,
Has rendered no Junes or Julys,
But touch we soft cross time and space,
For we've seen I do's in our eyes.

We've seen I do's and heard I do's,
We've felt I do's in our souls.
I think we long for the one I do,
That will make us feel whole.

Each night when we lay down to sleep, we entrust ourselves to fate or a higher power that we might awaken tomorrow. Sleep is a mandatory cyclical characteristic of our existence. We don't have to plan for it as it creeps upon us each night and renders hours as though they were minutes. In the pre-sleep state, just before we doze off, things can get a little silly sometimes. In this state we are half in the conscious state and half in the sleep state. My mind is usually very creative during this time which may last only a few minutes. The creative thoughts I have are usually nonsense and off the wall, but once in a while something serviceable emerges and surprises me.

As I am oft to do before I go to sleep at night, I whisper to Marilyn and tell her I love her, hoping that she will sense me and feel my love. It was during one of these pre-sleep states that I got the idea for the poem "For Now We Sleep". This poem is about our romance laying down to sleep for a while with the hope and trust that it will one day awaken and let us know that our love for each other still lives. As in the sleep that we all must yield to each night, we cannot know for certain that we will awaken tomorrow to all of the plans that we have made for our lives. Because of this, we trust and we pray.

During the sleep of our romance, Marilyn and I cannot see, hear and touch each other. This is because of the promise we made for sake of our need to heal our hearts and those of our families. My prayer is that we one day awaken from this self-imposed sleep state and walk out into the warm sun of our love, that our hearts might be full and faces bright with happiness.

"For Now We Sleep"

In the looming state of umbra,
Where shadowy silhouettes lurk,
Tomorrow's day is not defined,
And thoughts of reason not work.

Time itself is paced anew,
In this twilight and mystical state.
Reality filters through inane eyes,
Where one should not trust his fate.

Dreams profuse of the morrow,
In vivid imagery made.
No way for us to know for sure,
If we'll awaken to plans we laid.

Our windows are closed to the visage of each,
No sight, no sound, for now we sleep.

On Friday, March 10, 2000 at about 4:50 PM, Marilyn and I kissed for the first time. That kiss, although brief, was a brave and bold leap across what had appeared to be a wide divide. Marilyn had been insisting for weeks that we could not allow ourselves to get any closer than our attraction for each other had already drawn us. We were both trying to resist this natural chemistry we had for each other but neither of us was strong enough to resist it. That kiss sent us toppling head over heels down the path of a most wonderful two month romance.

Very few days went by without us sharing our sweet lips. We really loved holding each other, kissing slowly and tenderly. Whenever Marilyn got lost in a hot passion filled kiss, she would take a short gasping breath of air which let me know that I was pleasing her. Nothing pleased me more than knowing that I had pleased her.

I had wanted to kiss her for weeks and when that moment came, my heart pounded so hard that it scared me. She slipped her tongue in my mouth and slowly probed for the sweet passion that she needed from me. Her lips were so soft and the look in her eyes when we pulled away melted me into submission. At that moment, she had me.

The poem "The Kiss" is a reflection of what that kiss meant to me. It speaks of the restless nights I had thereafter and how time has done absolutely nothing to blur or fade the vivid memory of that moment. That moment is perfectly preserved in time and I cherish the memory every single day.

"The Kiss"

In annals, few things are,
In which I more delight,
Than our lips first met,
For, the world was right.

My heart well delighted,
Your body pressed to mine.
Though brief the encounter,
We tasted our sweet wine.

From this cup, we sipped a while,
To set free the pain of hearts.
Our chalice overflowed with love,
From end to our start.

My heart awakened that night.
My windows knew not sleep,
Pace did I till morning light,
Reflecting on this leap.

Now, great is my pain,
As your lips I so miss.
But vivid is always,
The moment of, The Kiss.

The love that Marilyn and I shared was heavenly. There was never a moment of angst between us. We were so tuned in and attentive to each other's needs. I found that I did not disagree with anything about her. In my eyes, we were the perfect match. She would tell me that I would not like her selfish nature. I kept looking for signs of this selfishness that she spoke of, but never saw any evidence of it. What I saw instead was a wonderfully giving woman who also knew how to receive and savor the love and attention that I showered upon her. Our love really was like a brilliant star that shined down from heaven. I believe that had we been able to stay together, our love would have gotten brighter as time went on. Our love would have been a shining example for all the world to see how a man and woman should love and care for each other.

On the evening before I wrote "A Star Fell From Heaven", I had sat on the deck looking out to the western sky thinking of Marilyn. I did not want to go inside that night because the sky was clear and the stars were so beautiful. It was so romantic imagining that she was sitting next to me whispering softly that she "just loved me so much". Looking at the majesty of God's beautiful stars, it dawned on me that the most beautiful star that God ever created was no longer in the heavens. That star was our love and the beauty of the sky was diminished by it not being there.

I pray that one day, God allows the light of our love to grace the beauty of the sky as it did for those two months from March to May.

"A Star Fell From Heaven"

A star fell from heaven,
When last you called my name.
That night in May, a sorrowed path,
Traversing the sky in flames.

On an ill wind, west it carried,
Beyond our known sorrow.
Into uncertainty it fell,
And with it, our tomorrow.

A star fell from heaven,
When last we fixed in our eyes,
The tender, gentle, loving hearts,
We found in our better sides.

A star fell from heaven,
Beyond our vista's sight.
And took with it, from now till then,
Heaven's most beautiful light.

One of my strong attributes is a single minded discipline that will not be compromised by anything or anyone. I have always been this way and it has served me well. It has really helped me through the most difficult time of trying to get over losing the love of my life. Even though I am strong, I am also human. There are days that I get tired and have to rest my weary spirit. I do this from time to time when I start to miss Marilyn too much and feel sorry for myself. I wonder what she is feeling and if she is missing me as I am her.

"The Mountain I Climb", is a comparison between my life every day since we broke up and the grueling prospect of climbing a mountain without being able to see the summit and not knowing where you are in the process. The weak of spirit would not be able to climb this mountain every day, but I draw strength from the climb because I know that I am one day closer to getting to the summer where the love of my life is waiting for me. I know that I am prepared to pay any price and sacrifice all that I have to this end for nothing has ever been so fulfilling as the love I have for Marilyn.

I learned many years ago that adversity is what strengthens us. Psychological and spiritual adversity are no different than physical adversity. They all tend to strengthen us if we do not give in and quit. We learn new things about ourselves and the metal we are made of. We find that we can handle much more than we thought and the more we oppose, the stronger we get. But we must oppose in these adversities in order to reap the benefits. With this in mind, I shall never give up on the mountain that I climb.

"The Mountain I Climb"

The mountain I climb is fraught with woe,
And I cannot see the summit.
But at its peak is the love we knew,
Before the night of plummet.

The mountain I climb is steep and cold,
It challenges my every step,
Testing my will to forge ahead,
And torturing my inner depth.

I'll not give up on the mountain I climb,
For it is my heart's desire.
I climb though I pain and ache in my core,
For the love at the top of this spire.

I cannot know when the summit I'll make,
As I cannot see clear to there.
So, closely I hold to the mountain I climb,
With courage and strength I dare.

When I look back at how and when Marilyn and I fell in love, I am amazed that we allowed it to happen at all. We spent so much time talking about how and why we could not allow ourselves to get involved, all the while growing closer. It was, at first, a bit scary because neither of us had ever found comfort in someone other than our mates. This was a very difficult thing for both of us. I have likened it to traveling through an uncharted forest. If you don't know what to expect, it can be foreboding. However, the weeks leading up to the beginning of our relationship were full of patience, listening, caring, compassion, understanding and tenderness. These weeks were the lush green meadows leading to our enchanted forest and allowed us to feel the comfort we needed to enter into our love.

When we fell in love, the forest revealed itself to us with all of the beauty that she and I had to bring. Life was so sweet and colorful with optimism and joy. Within our forest of love, we rested our weary hearts and soothed each other that our spirits be bound together for all of time to come. We looked deep inside of each other's wounded pasts to share our pain in a way that was cathartic. We exposed our deepest fears with each other and learned of new bravery within us. We shared our aspirations for the future and learned that we wanted the same things. We touched the untouched places deep within our souls and lingered a time upon the wispy promises we made to each other. We shared our hopes and dreams and planned to love each other forever.

Though we could not stay together within the forest, I believe that we are both still in the forest looking for the path that leads us back to we. I am still very much in love with Marilyn and I believe that she is still in love with me.

"Enchanted Forest"

When first we set upon our path,
Knowing not where it lead,
Our hearts controlled our firstly steps,
When it should have been our heads.

But on our path were lush and green meadows,
That led to an enchanted forest.
The forest consumed our mental will,
And made our decisions for us.

Amidst our forest were calm waters,
Where the butterflies seemed to know us.
We laid we down to rest our hearts,
On beds of fragrant flora.

The cooling calm and gentle breeze,
Burgeoned love in our hearts.
We shared our tender touches there,
That our spirits not ever part.

We've lost each other along the path,
But in the forest stay.
The forest is the love we share,
That shall never go away.

I had such a euphoric experience writing "Enchanted Forest", that the day afterwards was very depressing. While in the forest, I could see Marilyn and hear her voice. We spent hours lying in beautiful fields of flowers talking, kissing, laughing and gazing deeply in to each other's eyes. We were totally uninhibited because no one else was in our forest but us. We were in our own world and it was so beautiful. After completing this poem, I had to come back to the reality of my life without her. And so I began to get depressed.

I decided that these feelings and emotions were as valid as the joy I had experienced the day before and that I should capture them in verse also. "Where Are We" is the result of that thought. This poem begs to know if we are still in the forest of our love, searching to find each other. The second stanza paints a very painful and dark image of my perception of our once beautiful forest. It suggests a note of pessimism about whether we will be able to endure the dark storm that is looming in our love. Stanza three questions whether the beautiful truth that we shared was valid and worthy of having. And in stanza four, I am practically demanding from Marilyn to know if she is still in love with me as I state "I beg the question we".

At this point in the poem, I remember feeling angry. I wasn't angry at Marilyn, rather at the frustration and loneliness of not knowing whether we would one day find each other and return to the forest of our love. After completing this poem, I was physically and emotionally drained. I did not write again for three days as I needed time to heal from this experience.

"Where Are We"?

Where are we in this forest,
As hands no longer touch?
I look, I search, call out I do,
For the love I need so much.

Where are we Love, in night of day,
Enchantment yields to gloom?
Ebon shadows line the path,
As darker days to loom.

Where are we, that stood by sides,
Two friends yielding beauty of truth?
The miracle stars in eyes we saw,
A deeper definition of our youth.

We are we M, in this forest great,
I beg the question we?
Do you know where our future lies,
And what our fate will be?

Our relationship was so brief yet we experienced so much together. But there are so many simple things that we never got to experience, such as the changing of the seasons, a picnic, or running in the rain. We talked about so many things that we wanted to do together but our romance was cut short before we got to them. Many of our conversations were about different settings for making love. Making love was one of our favorite conversations because we both are very sexual and sensual people. One of the things that sticks in my mind is the fact that we did not get to share a winter together. I love winters because it is so much fun to snuggle together and stay warm. I felt so important when I put my arms around Marilyn but the thought of keeping her warm and safe as a result, sends chills through me. Making love in the winter is my favorite.

"Winter's Fire" was born of this kind of thinking. I amused myself one evening thinking how wonderful it would be for she and I to be locked away in a little cabin the winter with a cozy fire burning and no one else around to disturb our endless love sessions. There is snow on the ground symbolic of the purity of our love for each other. Inside of our cozy lair, we blissfully share our torrid passions all day and night screaming for mercy but with no ability to escape to opiate of our love.

While writing this poem, my passion for Marilyn was extremely hot and strong. I needed her so much then that I could almost feel me inside of her. I could hear her calling my name and taste her sweet lips. What a vision! I wondered to myself if she could feel me while I was feeling her so intensely. I wondered if in her solitude, she gave these kind of thoughts to us and longed for the day when we could make them happen.

"Winter's Fire"

Winter brings its chilling winds.
Outside is cold and grey.
Our hearts are warmed with thoughts of love,
As we while the day away.

Snuggle we close, the fire in our hearts,
The flame of our love never dies.
Peer we through the window our souls,
Where the beauty of our love resides.

Wrapped in love, the blanket we,
Absorbing the crackling fire,
Our lips make sweet the taste of wine,
As we yield our passions desire.

We tend our fire and stoke our fire,
It's wonderfully beautiful flame,
It burns intensely through the night,
As we scream each other's name.

Take well we do the warmth we make,
From fire that burns within,
Eternal love, our winter's fire,
This day until the end.

As Marilyn's birthday nears, I am feeling more and more anxious about contacting her. I know that we are not supposed to do this but I am really hurting inside with this decision. I cannot decide whether, to do so, would make her happy or angry. I know that I really wish she would call me. Her voice would be like a drink of water to a man who is parched of thirst in the desert. I have longed for her so long now that I am hearing her voice in my head and it is of some concern to me. Again I am questioning my sanity.

"Hunger In My Soul" is about me questioning myself as to why I am allowing this misery of not having her, to be a part of my life. I have always been a very strong willed individual with excellent control of my mind. My resolute self-discipline was further sharpened and polished by four years as a drill sergeant in the Air Force. Why then can I not move on without her in my life and find some sense of normalcy?

The answer to that question is found in the reason Marilyn and I fell in love in the first place. It is because we had spent so many years in hunger of that something, which made life complete. That connection to another person that fully understood your wants, needs, and fears and took so much joy in attending to them. We were both the perfect keys for the locked doors of true happiness within our hearts. It is not possible for me to walk away from the one person that filled me up with happiness.

Her love was like a feast at the bountiful table of life. She filled me to satisfaction every day and I hungered not. Today, there is a hunger in my soul and it cannot be satiated without her.

"Hunger In My Soul"

Who binds thusly with angst,
Except he who knows not will,
Of matters Eros with the fairer,
Who would buy my hand hold still?

For sake of our morrow depose,
That our lights not shown on each.
For want of righteous sake,
Turn under, the beauty of our breach.

Attempting and tempting my fate,
With gauntlet narrow and steep.
Of challenged frayed measure my courage,
A darkened vigil my soul keeps.

Alas, impoverished spirit,
Rend thee from the whole.
Find the fest that fills again,
The unsatiated hunger in my soul.

"In Blue Fields Lay We Down" is one of my favorites in this collection. It was inspired by reading "Enchanted Forest", a previous poem in this collection. While reading this poem, I imagined the beautiful colors of the flora there. I had a vision of an expansive field near the lake in our forest. That field was covered with nothing but small, densely growing blue flowers. Blue flowers are somewhat rare in nature. Horticulturists have succeeded in hybridizing them but, everything, in our forest is natural and un-touched by man. The beauty and rarity of the blue flowers is symbolic of our love. It was special and so beautiful just like the field of blue flowers.

The surreal setting of our forest's image in my mind created mystery and intrigue. These elements contribute to imagination and wonder. For the creative literary mind, this is the magic formula for expressive writing. Marilyn is inspiration enough for me, however the symbolism of our forest of love is vividly colorful and bright. I sometimes am overwhelmed by what I am feeling when I have been in the forest for an extended time.

A common theme in this collection of poetry is the soft and gentle nature of our relationship. Another theme is that, though we are apart, we still love each other very much. We long for the day when we will be able to return to each other and live in our mystical forest of deep and soulful love forever and in blue fields lay we down.

"In Blue Fields Lay We Down"

Though our vistas vast,
And our travels far,
That we've seen the corners,
Compare not where we are.

This place that our spirts share,
Cannot be traveled to.
Nor can it be born by others.
It exists between, for me and you.

Upon its open meadow,
In hearts as ours, bound,
Time yields it's pretty wings,
And in blue fields lay we down.

Lay we down in blue fields,
Lay we down our souls.
That our hearts make one sound.
And in this place, become whole.

"Storm In The Wilderness" is a poem about the painful time Marilyn and I must endure between our first love and the next. I have likened this time to a storm in the wilderness because they both evoke fear and uncertainty. The emotional elements are so powerful and we have no control of them just as we have no control of the elements of a storm. We are powerless to do anything but ride the storm out and pray for the best outcome. And yet we are aware of the benefits the storm will leave behind.

Beyond each storm is a fresh rebirth and renewal of the wondrously beautiful aspects of life. It is the darkness and violence of the storm which makes us appreciate the new bath of sunlight and the colorful flora which follows. They lift our spirits in a way which cannot be achieved otherwise. The rains give drink to the parched earth and reconstitutes our souls in so doing. All that was, becomes again and love springs forth out of the lonely wilderness. The storm is the price that we pay for the beauty of all there is, including true, deep, soulful love which lasts a lifetime. Those who successfully endure the storm are blessed and strengthened in a special way.

In our storm are brilliant flashes of memories of her smiling deep into my soul, followed by the thunderous sound of her sweet voice whispering she "just loves me so much". In between the flashes lie the roaring background sound of my soul's tears raining down upon the fertile ground of what will be our future if we both weather the storm. Each day and night, I pray for her and in so doing, pray for us.

"Storm In The Wilderness"

In the distance, heaven speaks,
Of a presence to come,
Of renewal of that which was,
Of love yesterday from.

Yet, fore all is new,
Must come rain no less.
Before eternal beauty,
Comes a storm in the wilderness.

No sorrow accorded the storm.
Being in it is part of life.
For beyond its winds of change,
Is the oasis void of strife.

The wilderness and we are of the storm,
And all its mystical sounds.
Tomorrow is a day of growth,
Where truth and beauty are found.

The night before Marilyn's birthday, I did not sleep. I tossed and turned until I couldn't take it anymore. I got up, went to my office and began writing. Before the sun rose, I had completed two poems to commemorate her birthday. The first, "This Day" was a struggle to write because I was feeling bad about not being with her on her birthday. Being awake and alone in the A.M. hours when the city is asleep is conducive to hearing your deepest thoughts. I wanted to call Marilyn on her birthday so much. I wanted her to have these two poems that I had written. I wanted to know that on this special day, she was so happy. I wanted to be a part of the reason she was happy. Writing a happy and cheerful poem when I felt so down was very difficult. Once I figured out how to put my feelings aside and feel what I wanted her to feel, the words came easier. I saw the most beautiful day of the entire year, warm, sunny and air sweet with the happy sound of birds singing to and about her. When I finished this poem, I realized that Marilyn makes every day of my life beautiful because she is a part of who I am now.

"In Quiet Moments" is a reflection of how it is the quietest of times of my life that I feel Marilyn so much more intensely. I can give the thoughts and memories of she and I my undivided attention for lengthy periods of time. When I close my eyes and listen to my heartbeat, I can see her eyes possess me as she did when we held each other and kissed. I hear her breathing and then we merge into oneness. I feel as if I'm in a trance of sorts and I am at total peace. Given the pain of my reality, I wish I could retreat to this special place and never return.

Better still would be for her to return to my reality.

"This Day"

This day is Marilyn beautiful,
Full of sunshine and joy.
The birds are singing extra sweet,
For the wonderful woman you are.

You surely must be smiling now,
For the air is fresh and sweet.
Your gentle breeze whispers soft,
Caressing the day complete.

The angels sing a chorus sweet,
In heavens up above,
From end to end of the universe,
About your special love.

Your special love is in me,
It never goes away.
It lets me know that it is you,
Who makes so beautiful this day.

"In Quiet Moments"

In quiet moments,
Your smile reflects back at me,
From the still surface of life,
Warming with memories of we.

In quiet moments,
Your voice I hear, a rhapsody singing soft,
Gentle, making sweet the air we breathe,
Easing our weariness off.

In quiet moments,
I look into your eyes for love.
Our spirits meld and live again,
Giving to each, the other of.

In quiet moments,
I hold your loving hand,
And place upon my heart a promise,
To always be your forever man.

"Calm Waters"

Calm waters I see of thee,
And want again jump in,
To give myself forevermore,
To love of Marilyn.

Beware, I must, the glassy sheen,
Smooth, calm and clear.
For it belies what's underneath,
A raging current severe.

Calm waters are so beautiful
They mirror the love of we.
But in their depths a current flows.
Towards some destiny.

It's irresistible nature,
Does mesmerize my soul.
My fate I tempt upon its berth,
To let consume me whole.

I have always had reverence for the cycles and rhythms of life and our world. These cycles are God's intricately beautiful works. They are accurate and reliable beyond the feeble and inconsistent nature of man. Indeed, I am humbled by the beauty and scale of these rhythms. My favorite is the rising and setting of our sun. I've tried for many years to decide for myself which is the more beautiful but must admit that I cannot choose. They have unique characteristics which make them equally beautiful. Together, they are equal components of one of the perfect cycles of our world.

On the day that I wrote "A Perfect Circle", I awakened early before daylight so as to watch the sun rise. I do this often as it allows me time to be with God and talk before I start my day. This day was a Sunday and I sat for more than an hour, taking in the symphony of a most beautiful sunrise. It was complete with the songs of birds, squirrels playing in the lawn and trees and a gently soothing wind that God sent to remind me that He still loved me. I asked God to protect Marilyn and to bless her with health and happiness as I do every day.

These types of settings are very conducive to creative writing and so the inspiration for "A Perfect Circle" was born. My idea for this poem was to try to weave the beautiful tapestry of our love into the beautiful aspects of a sunrise and sunset. Utilizing metaphorical comparatives such as "pastel smile" and "billowy images" help to communicate the like beauties of our love and the sun's cycle. In this poem, our love is an integral part of the cycle. Indeed, one of us is the sunrise and the other the sunset. I just can't figure out which is which. It doesn't matter though. We contribute equally to the beauty of our love.

"A Perfect Circle"

The sun rises on pristine images
Of pastel smiles and breezes soft,
Stirring our winds to life,
Carrying our thoughts aloft.

Soaring above all which is under foot,
Sol arcs toward tomorrow,
Beyond billowy images of our love,
As gleeful youth our spirits borrow.

We linger a time upon our memories,
As Sol pursues the distant horizon,
Ushering the cooling evening winds,
Which our parched souls rely on.

Cool nights give way to another sun rise,
As the sun again creates its miracle,
Balancing the lonely nights,
Making complete, our perfect circle.

"But Not For A Friend" is very nearly a poem about thanks and gratitude. Marilyn taught me so many things about myself that I did not know. I think the most important thing that she taught me was that I was worthy of deep soulful love that asks for nothing but the same in return. She softened my walls and penetrated the shield that I had around my heart. The shield had been there for many years because as a child I learned not to trust people. No doubt because I was duped so many times by other children. My distrust of people caused me to take an exceedingly long time to allow anyone to get close to me. Even with Marilyn, it took two months of daily talking with her for me to begin to feel comfortable. This compares to years, if ever, for most people that I meet.

I came to know that she had a painful childhood as did I but for very different reasons. We bonded quickly because we both understood each other's pain and knew how to sooth it. Out of the very fertile soil of our understanding grew a strong friendship which blossomed into the beautiful flower of our love.

The moment that I knew I was in love with her came when I realized that she and her love for me was what my life had been missing. She communicated her love for me in so many ways. My favorites were the way she touched me soft and gently and most of all, the way she looked into my eyes. Her eyes spoke from her soul and when she did, she owned me. The experience of loving and being loved by her has been worth the pain of losing her. To know that I was worthy of that level of love was an awakening. It adds dimension to the way that I look and feel about myself, even today. For this I am eternally grateful to her.

"But Not For A Friend"

I am the past desiring your future,
But your memory is my now.
I struggle with what is best for us,
While managing my sanity somehow.

Though I've not your hand to hold,
I cling fastly to the thoughts of thee.
For surely the sun rises in the west,
And sets wherever you be.

Loving you the depth and breadth of my soul
Has validated a worthy existence of my life,
Rendering color and texture from the palette,
Of the woman who would otherwise by my wife.

But not for a friend should I remain loveless,
And find not the path to fulfillment.
As in the glow of your presence,
The love we share is heaven sent.

On the day that I wrote "The Cloud I'm In", I was deeply depressed. Enough that I felt physically poor. I had a low-grade headache and my vision was impaired. The muscles in my upper back and shoulders were knotted into a tense ball. My greatest desire was to be undisturbed but of course, I was at work and that was not possible. I was in a very bad mood and that was the polar opposite of my personality. I pride myself on being personable, friendly and helpful with every person that I come in contact with in my work environment. To lose my temper with the people who rely on me to be up and bring them up when they are not feeling one hundred percent would have been disastrous. I kept thinking that if I could just make it to lunch without exploding at someone, everything would be fine. Lunchtime is when I'd write and writing poetry to Marilyn always made me feel better. It was cathartic and very good therapy for the frequent bouts of depression I experienced after she and I parted. In a very real way, I felt as if I was communicating with Marilyn when I wrote poetry to her.

In this poem, the first three stanzas are lamentations of my condition without her in my life. On this day I felt as if I was walking around in a cloud aimlessly moving with no idea of where I was headed. I remember feeling fear for not knowing what was coming at me and paranoia about what my co-workers were seeing in my behavior. Some days were very difficult to cope with and this was a particularly bad one. As usual, at some point in my writing, I began to focus on the joy that Marilyn brought to my life and the sweet memory of her voice. The last two stanzas area reflective of this change in my mood as optimism once again sprang forth. After lunch, I was in a much better mood and that much deeper in love with her.

"The Cloud I'm In"

Days on end without sight,
Nights make not me a friend.
I see not colorful birds I hear,
Because of the cloud I'm in.

I ask of me my destiny,
I measure the man within.
I see not vistas yonder there,
For sight the cloud I'm in.

The want my heart is crystal clear,
Your love my spirit depends,
But cannot find your hand to hold,
For sight the cloud I'm in.

You're my sun, your love the warmth,
That push away this cloud.
I want to see the birds with you,
Singing our love aloud.

"Our Journey"

We journeyed we along the path,
Beyond our doubts and fears.
The morrow's promise knew not end,
For love we held so dear.

This loving journey traveled we,
A path of parallel,
To other mates we early chose,
Who did not serve us well.

Surrendered we to that we found,
This path in hearts alike,
To tender kiss the pain therein,
For time to heal our strife.

Though very brief, our journey was,
It well did serve our hearts.
While separately we walk today,
Our spirits are never apart.

"Symbols Of Our Sacrifice"

Sad sunsets without smiles,
An ache in the backdrop of life,
Arms that hold not warmth of we,
Symbols of our sacrifice.

Memories of us that fill the days,
Nights that are much too long,
Dreams we made uncertain be,
Heartaches that go on and on.

A longing to know the other's day,
A chance encounter we might,
Thoughts of us in all we see,
Symbols of our sacrifice.

Our other's hearts, though content,
Do feel the squeeze, this vise,
For they know well the truth we bear,
Symbols of our sacrifice.

No tender touch, no sweet, sweet lips,
No baritone silk in your ear,
No wonder we unhappy be,
True love we sacrificed Dear.

"On Wings of Wind"

I cast my voice, whispering,
On westward winds so soft,
Her name I speak in gentle style,
A prayer I send aloft.

Please, oh winds, do carry,
This prayer I send her way.
I pray dear God to lift her life,
On wings of wind each day.

I pray oh Lord that she may soar,
To slip these earthly bonds,
That she may know a deeper peace,
And love of life beyond.

I pray dear God you hold her near,
And nestle her spirit within.
Give her life the lift it needs,
To soar on wings of wind.

Touch her days with golden lift,
A beacon of one true friend,
Let her life be smooth of flight,
On wings of wind, Amen.

"Marilyn, Marilyn, Marilyn"

When I whisper your name,
My heart sings soft,
A melody of perfect notes,
That chases my misery off.

Marilyn, Marilyn, Marilyn,
My heart loves to sing,
Harmonic chords of loving thoughts,
With pure and golden ring.

The birds all stop to listen,
This heavenly beautiful song.
Then join to add their chorus,
As they lovingly sing along.

A crescendo we build, our chorus,
What a wonderfully beautiful tone,
Marilyn, Marilyn, Marilyn,
We sing you all day long.

"Magic Words"

There is much, much magic,
In words I give to you,
For they convey my deepest me,
And love for you so true.

Our darkened moments travel,
To distant corner flee.
Magic words make possible,
That which could not be.

From somewhere deep within,
Magic words come to me,
Passion thoughts of feelings,
Painting pastel imagery.

The best words yet are in me,
Secured for that day,
When once again our eyes do meet,
And speak that our hearts do say.

"Where Truth Lies"

Tis an age old conundrum,
With optly abundant whys,
That tax the agile and fragile minds,
In quest of where truth lies.

What is real and what is not,
A simple postulate yeah?
Yet seek we this within this realm,
Until our dying day.

Somewhere 'tween our voices say,
And what our hearts do feel,
The pure unblemished pearl of life,
Is throned upon glorious reveal.

That we might seek to bind of hearts,
And find the pearl in eyes,
Is greatly cause for hope in we,
For therein is where truth lies.

"Whisper On My Pillow"

Silent, still, darkened room,
Sleep takes my weary mind.
Whisper I my final thoughts,
On this day I leave behind.

I whisper on my pillow
Your lovely name each night,
That visions of your smile,
Dream that I might.

I whisper on my pillow,
I love you deeply Dear,
And pray that your return,
To my arms draw near.

I pray your light shines,
Upon my face again,
Warming the unending love,
I hold for you within.

Whisper on my pillow,
In dreams, my ear you say,
Your love of me, yet you hold,
That never fades away.

"My Darkest Hour"

Resolve for living is extremely poor,
An unfriendly, bitter wind blows,
Against what courage the sparrow knows,
As strength are rend for sure.

It is bitterly cold in this empty nest,
Where many tears fall to freeze.
Snow packs the branches of my lonely tree,
As prayers goes for final rest.

Days are unbearable, long are the nights,
Chilling the psyche and soul.
Prayer goes to God, for delivery whole,
Into His loving light.

For in this cold, there blooms no flower,
And each day begins with my darkest hour.

"For Sanity's Sake"

The grip I've lost on my writing pen,
And fear my sanity too.
My days are increasingly filled my love,
With thoughts of no one but you.

I look for you wherever I go,
Near and far and wide,
Imagining that wherever I walk,
You're always by my side.

I've called your name so many times,
You've started answering back.
The loving conversations we have,
Are what my reality lacks.

I'll save what's left of my weary mind,
On the chance you'll one day return.
And nestle close in my heart again,
Where the flame of our love yet burns.

In this hazy state and desperate retreat,
A painful decision I make,
To retire my pen with you my love,
Au revoir, for sanity's sake.

What follows are works written by Luster Lewis that were not part of his collection of 54.

"A Daffodil"

I've fashioned myself a daffodil,
To quit the worldly norm.
My thoughts ethereal, abstract verse
That bloom uncommon poem.

I found myself in early time,
The state ennui with man.
Retreat did I from crowds of they,
To a wondrous lyrical land.

Bode did I among my thoughts,
A time to hone my skills,
To capture deeply passionate verse,
This narcissus daffodil.

And as the opiate upon my mind,
It wrest me from my kin
To hold me there amongst my thoughts,
No common prose let in.

I've fashioned myself a daffodil,
Alone, in love with my thoughts,
But wish that I could average be,
That metrical verse not haunt.

"A Flower In The Desert"

On a very special occasion,
A beautiful flower springs forth
In an otherwise barren desert.
Its true beauty is magnified by the stark
and extreme contrast of its surroundings.
That the flower exists at all in such a
place is a testament to its unseen
strength, adaptability and resolve.
To be in the presence of such beauty
Is one of life's greatest joys.

I wonder however,
Does the flower know?
Is it aware of how it improves all
that is around it?
Does it sense my absolute joy?
Does it know how empty this
place would be without it?
Sad is the thought of you not
knowing the beauty of your presence.

In the solitude of your essence,
Smile deeply and sense my admiration.

"An Elegy to Doubt" (Italian Sonnet)

Oh surly doubt, a rogue thou areth,
A blackguard of ill repute,
When in the dark a pillaged loot,
Thy make in lover's hearts.
Creeping up from moggy mires,
With odious ways contempt,
Rending light, and spirits gimp,
Quelling their passion'd fires.
Would that they know better days,
When truth supplants thy will.
And overtures there gleefully,
Hold guard thy caustic ways.
But in the glad, thy killing fields,
Lay slain their trust by thee.

"A Third Bird"

A brightly crested songstress
Once, in their old tree lit
But to the east his mate was turned,
And caught not wind of this.
And so his tired heart and eyes,
Turned west to her new song,
Which held him spelled a little while,
That must have been too long.
Descend did he, a lofty perch
Of oh so many years,
To listen sweetly to her song,
And taste her painful tears.
But in her song were notes so sharp,
They pierce his heart and soul,
Which turned him back towards the east
To warm his mate so cold.
And now he nests a lower perch,
No song from his mate is heard,
Their fate forever thusly turned,
By the song of a third bird.

"At This Moment" (Sonnet)

At this moment, a year ago hence,
    Two Hearts touched, by way of lips,
    Giving life to the beautiful friendship
That endures what has happened since.
At this moment, I ache in my soul,
    To retake that first kiss,
    To linger and lavish the lips I so miss,
And again, in my arms each, we hold.
At this moment, my heart beats that song,
    Of passion filled notes,
        And trembling bars,
That filled the air we floated on,
    Carrying heats as wind blown boats,
        That quit the sea to
mingle with the stars.

"Bittersweet Hour"

Not so subtle are the throws,
That in our achings keep,
From when we part of tender kiss,
And make our spirits weep.

For such a march of time doth pang,
A gnawing in our core,
Yet bittersweet the knowing that,
Our lips will touch once more.

If knew not we the love we share,
That make this lonely hour,
The throws and pangs that we now keep,
Would bide no lofty tower.

For in that tower our hearts do dwell,
And seek each other's fold,
Which make the hours that our lips touch,
Be that of precious gold.

Then hold this hour of ache and angst,
In bittersweet regard,
For soon our lips will kiss again,
And willst this hour discard.

"Bitter Winds Of December"

In the chill of my dim and empty room,
fending the rage of winter's song,
I sit alone and contemplate
warmth of yesterdays gone.
The incessant winds push
against memories of yore,
and the shivering chill avers,
that yesterday is nevermore.
The warmer days have ceded
to a snow covered roof,
a pallid shell of its former self,
as embers gray doth the spirit reproof.
Cracked, the dried veneer
does not the warmth of love hold,
as the bitter winds of December
lay bare my empty soul.
The winter song howls, swirling, encircling
the veiled remnants of yesterday,
that now creak with piercing drafts.
As to this season, its end I pray.

"But For Love"

But for thy breath, would I not breath,
Utterances of passionate thought,
Nor gird my reluctant courage,
To uncover in me what God has wrought.

But for thy distilled sweetness, would I bitter be.
For that which you so freely give,
Nectar, your pure and sweet truth,
Make upon each day, my reason to live.

But for thy delicate hands, would I hold naught.
And keeping with furrowed brow,
Would I wander aimlessly, amid dim moments,
In quest of thy lasting vow.

But for thy loving eyes, could I not see
Our truth, surrendering all doubt,
To pledge in souls, in hearts, forever.
And by a pledge, are we the other, never without.

About this poem: For my Marilyn, whose love I could never live without.

"Calm within My Hands"

When the stormy seas rage within,
And the throws of life toss you about,
When all hope seems at end,
And the swells engulf you with doubt,
I'll be there, to calm they seas,
And make a smile upon your heart.
My light is that of luster,
I'll shine in your darkest dark.
I'm always there, awaiting your want,
Your desire, your passion for living,
Needing but your simplest command,
That I might know the joy in giving.
Rest easy upon my shores,
Musing the grains of sand.
Be at peace with placid thoughts,
For the calm within my hands.

"Cold Sleep"

'Tis oft a trifle we see,
Of that which really is,
In oceans dark,
Where wounded hearts live.
In fathoms deep,
Fractured and bitterly cold,
In want, I weep,
Forlorned for love to hold.
In depths, hidden
Away from view,
Are leagues there, smitten,
Forever charged thereto.
But alas, in silence deep,
Adrift on lingering way,
The heart yields to cold sleep,
And bids adieu this day.

About this poem: In the bitterly cold, deep waters of lost love, the heart rathers death than the continued experience of life's pain.

"Empty Shore" (Italian Sonnet)

On an empty shore, in a quiet place,
Sinking in pallid grains of time,
Lay a spirit, ineffably divine,
A featureless visage of face.
Lay thereto footsteps that trace,
So brilliant a love sublime,
Left by tideless sea, confined
To the stillness of this barren waste.
There blow not winds for avian to loft
Songs upon heavy air that hang,
Nor counter-roar of relentless tide.
Count we too, victims oft,
Who's hearts broke the quiet and sang
But in the motionless sea now reside.

"Dad's Tools"

When I was just a boy so young,
I played with my father's tools,
Crafting toys and playful things,
Like scooters, oh so cool.

I found the key to his shed,
Where he kept his saw.
When he was gone I'd enter there,
And violate his law.

For Dad forbade me in his shed,
To tamper with his things.
He laid the law down sternly there,
And warned, his belt would sting.

But driven by a passion deep,
To conjure and create,
I entered there his tools to use,
His law to violate.

Many a day I worked his saw,
And honed my skills so fine,
I loved the sound of ripping boards,
And wafting scent of pine.

But came a day when I was tired,
And forgot to store his tools.
The sun did rise upon their rust,
Borne by the morning dews.

Sure enough his words were true,
His belt did surely sting.
You'd think that after once or twice,
I'd leave alone his things.

Many a night he'd find that I
Had entered in his shed,
And there he'd stand, awakening me,
Whipping me in my bed.

But what my Dad could never know,
Was that I could not stop,
For in me burned a passion deep,
That to this day burns hot.

This thing in me that God hath wrought,
It must be satisfied.
It lives and breathes each painful tear,
Shed in those midnight cries.

My Dad has passed away from life,
And with him went his shed.
But he's in every board I cut,
As in my heart and head.

About this poem: I wrote this poem as a tribute to my dad, Roy Lewis, who passed away suddenly on January 28th, 1999. I never imagined I'd miss him so very much. His spirit lives and breathes in every project I construct. And I choose to believe he is very proud of me.

"Feathers Of The Eagle"

They slipped the bonds to soar with the eagle
as new plumes in the bloodied pinions,
lofting as angels, that we mere mortals
would long endure, holding their bravery in awe,
while yearning similitudes of courage.

That the spirit of our great nation was measured
by hideous trial and found to be not lacking,
bore testament to the powerful currents that
ever flow beneath our patience and calm.

That we buttressed our national resolve and
leveraged our pain, forging unbreakable bonds
within our family, served notice that our strength
is born of courage. And our courage is amplified
many folds in acts against us, well iterating
what this family means to itself
and indeed, the world.

Woe be unto they who awakened the ire of this
Gentle giant by smite. For
though our patience long
and temperance full, we spare
not a single heartbeat
in a full measure of justice for
those who would soil our
skies with hatred, and defile the
feathers of the eagle.

About previous poem: My tribute to the men and women who perished on September 11, 2001. As a patriot and proud American, I live their sacrifice in every breath I take.

∞

"Finding Thy Pearl"

Mired in tangled thoughts,
Of part time revelry,
Fleet a glimpse of wonder well,
That cloak in thy mystery.

Thriving in darkened hours,
Revealing and healing the night.
In the recesses of uncertainty,
Glow the love of thy pearl's light.

Try that I might uncover full,
The illusive and beautiful treat,
Thy furtive pearl eludes me well,
Fending my sight complete.

But give not way to acquiesce,
In quest of lighting my world,
That would the fullness of the day,
Be lit by finding the pearl.

"Forlorn"

I pine thy fragrant thoughts my love,
Your pretty name in my screen,
Longing to know shared moments as one,
And for this, a heart that would sing.

But I've found no ardor in the frigid clime,
Of a day without the light,
Which doth my will test surely for want,
Of one word, to sooth this plight.

But alas, this day slips into dusk,
Where the sea quenches all desire,
Chilling the residue of quelled heartaches,
And the embers of our early morn's fire.

"Gallant Knight"

Do you see when musing,
The gallant knight so near,
Who's patient style and wispy touch,
Do slay your inner fears?

Do you see his love of thee,
Save thy troubled hour,
Which make upon thy heart a smile,
And glow thy inner flower?

Make note, his tempered saber,
When stand he next to you,
To slay thy toothy dragons there,
Out in the meadows blue.

Keep well Dear Heart, the hand of he,
Who smite thy troubles down.
For in this day of shallow men,
Few gallant knights are found.

"Gold Boy"

The sun rose on a golden boy,
When eyes and hearts sought peace,
A golden time of promise and joy
In quarters not before this lease.

Old thoughts were bathed in hope,
His days of men and strife,
Shaped his strength and will to cope,
To live his exemplary life.

Though darkened skies loomed the edge,
His gold by light ever shown,
To bathe the seeds his loins pledge,
Till they were fully grown.

And shield their faces that he might,
Till strength in their hearts and hands,
Reflect his will and golden light,
Beyond the Hallum lands.

Though set the sun a wintry day,
To rest his light so fine,
We own the gift of his life to say,
His gold boy light yet shines.

"Grieved"

Last night I grieved into the dawn,
For want of a quiet hour,
That knew not thoughts of yesterday,
Which loft in cloudy towers.

My darkened room did silence make,
Which fastly gave way,
To sight and sound of loving thoughts,
Before this lonely day.

The ebon glom set upon my brow,
As my eyes sealed out the night,
But my heart would not the day complete,
Without thy loving light.

And so I grieved into the dawn,
Feeling the stillness weep,
And prayed that in the coming day,
My broken heart find sleep.

"Her Breeze"

Upon warm moments, her bouquet swirls,
Into midday eddies, capturing my mind,
Spinning to dizzying states,
As time itself unwinds.
Helpless in tow, within her wake,
My possessed manhood follow,
Without strength of will
Aflutter, like so many swallows.
As upon her breeze, I go,
With heart, an unmarked while,
And I close my senses, save that of smell,
To breath the warmth of her style,
And chance the honey upon her lips,
In fleeting moments, thence,
To make sweet the heat of her breeze,
That fill my passion sense.

"His Flower"

I asked God for a flower,
Instead He gave me you.
And in my most quiet hour
Wherein my breath were shallow,
He bade me care for thee
With tender hands and heart,
That I might know the fullness
Of thy sweet nectar.

And therein I pledged thee
My most attentive care,
That would nurture they stem strong,
They petals soft, and fragrance of spirit.
Thence have I righteously given
Profound thanks to my Lord,
For the gift of His flower in you,
And the joy you bring to my life.

"His Masterpiece"

I have lifted sleepy eyelids
To many a yawning dawn
And mused the avian minstrels
Who hold not their tongues
For glee of morning glow.

I have gazed into that moment,
A singularity of total peace
That signifies the gift of rebirth
and waded, fully immersed,
in its ultimate beauty.

I have given humbly, my meagerness
in awe, and wed my soul to its grandeur.
Bewildered by the bliss therein,
my eyes have filled my heart
with its breathtaking flight.

And oft I have folded into that quiet
place, the timbre of which is ever calm.
without song stirred winds, but dreamy
light, to touch the hand of He who would
Place me in the moment of His Masterpiece.

"Hounds At My Heels"

I am but moments short this day,
And briefly I must be,
For sooth the hounds be at my heels,
Their prying eyes might see.

No moments still in hours past,
Hath I known pure peace,
In quest therein of solitude,
That doth my words not fleece.

But save thee there a coming time,
That yield not acquiesce,
For surely I shall shake the hounds
That doth my patience test.

"I Brought You Light"

The light of my life arose in the west,
Borne by a bird of silver wings,
Lofting on air of a winsome song,
That in my heart ever sings.

As the light ascends to places high,
Pushing back the cold of night,
An omnipresent voice whispers in my soul,
"I'm home my love, and with me,
I brought you light".

I brought you light for places dark
Within you that need my glow,
And once again made nearer we,
To that which we know "we know".

I brought you light this early morn,
To help you clearly see,
Our love ascending in the west,
And nearer me to thee.

"If Ever" (Italian Sonnet)

If ever within a moment sublime,
When wing'd thoughts well hover,
Capturing vividly one or the other,
Sight or sound of a bygone time,
Or ever within a tortured line
Of thought that give not cover,
There tolls a bell for another
That haunts thy mental clime.
If ever one find within thy state,
No have or retreat,
To pass the time so idly by,
And savor the wine to sate,
Thy heart controls, with every beat,
Thy cloistered mind that sighs.

About this poem: In the aftermath of true love lost, the mind can be quite rational but often the heart will not behave.

"I Saw Time Stand Still"

I saw time stand still,
One moody morn in May,
And witness love, there hold in,
Breath for a latter day.

I saw time stand still,
That morn you called my name,
To say you shared our secret love,
That life not be the same.

I saw time stand still,
When dark did cloak our world,
And entered we a paradigm shift,
As realities vector swirled.

I saw time stand still,
The fabric of space did tear,
When wrest our eyes apart from we,
To vanquish our love so fair.

I saw time stand still,
The day we walked away,
My heart did fold within itself,
To quit the light of day.

"I Wish"

I wish to always feel the silky butterfly float lightly
on golden currents that emanate from our touch.
I wish to rein the winds that
they whisper our names,
drawing so lightly, as a bow, across
the strings of our hearts.
I wish to walk within the light of
your smile in all my moments,
be they night of day, your hand in mine,
defining me, giving birth to who I am.
I wish to know the greatest depth in
thy soul for having been there
and placing upon thy heart my
essence, my spirit, my all.
I wish to take upon my shoulders,
the weight of your worry
and champion your happiness
into endless sunlit morns.
I wish for you to know the depth of
my love for thee, that bind
thy most defeated fears and lay
them at the calm river which
flows ever in me. At that river, I wish
them away that your feet not
scrape their brambled tooth and spill
not thy honey upon the path.
I wish to spend eternity fixed in your
presence, not one moment
away and never again needing to say, "I wish".

"Midnight Chimes"

The night air is a symphony,
Of windy painted lilt,
A rhapsody in ecstasy,
Replete with baritone silk.

The throaty blow, seductive clef,
And lusty moans so low,
Do twine amid the heated air,
That weave we to and fro.

To softly stroke the midnight chimes,
Our symphony well alive,
With vibrant, quivering, tensioned pitch,
That shiver our souls inside.

And lose the bar and measure count,
On into morning light,
But find allergro passion'd winds,
In midnight chimes delight.

So soft we now, with morning glow,
To leave the lilt behind.
Yet burn we fast the light of day,
For want of midnight chimes.

"Midnight Mourn"

The Mocking bird cries at night
for the love that does not return,
and thusly fains not sleep.
Her song is from within, and deep,
endless, without shame or fear
for the world to hear.
She wails her love and care,
for the sun will not rise without him near.
As the dark is as day, the day is as night,
when she has called in fright,
a plea his return upon
their nest to light.
Another joining of their souls
to sing a sunrise right.
For him she cries from the
darkened nest of their yesterdays.
For the morrow's heartache she cannot bear.
She is full of loathing and fear
for what could be her final song,
by ill or intent.

"Mind Body And Soul"

That I have given my mostly thoughts,
To these many days,
And sought expressive love of thee
In oh so many ways.

That I have watched each setting sun,
Westward of our love,
And given prayer for your return,
To our God above.

That I have held your full embrace,
And known the joy therein,
And felt your body's heat pass through
The space between us thin.

That I have felt your chest to mine,
And taste thy budding flower,
To make my passion burn inside,
And want of you devour.

That I have wagered eternity,
For want of love of thee,
And tempt the fate my soul therein,
To know our destiny.

That I have spoken all these things,
When taken as a whole,
Is truth I love thee deeply Dear,
Mind, body and soul.

"Mom's Love"

Unyielding in her resolve
To be and give her best,
That we, who call her Mom,
Will, in her arms, find rest
From those thousands
Of aches and pangs
That pierce our days
With venomous fangs.
But for the champion that she is,
Protecting us from the world,
And sometimes from ourselves,
When logic and sanity we hurl
Through some illusionary port,
Beyond which we mistakenly reason
Our freedom from her watchful eye,
Would we but lose fully, our season.
Resolutely though, she stands
In the midst of her own pain,
Pouring her soul devoutly into ours,
Sacrificing her wordly gain
That we should know
A fuller measure of life,
In length, breadth and joy,
And know not piercing strife.

About this poem: Mom's love teaches us civility and temperance, insulating us from the lowly barbarian instincts of our ancestral vestiges. Mom's love is special and as vital as a heartbeat or a sunrise to our continued existence. It is one of God's greatest gifts to human kind. Cherish her and her love in every breath you take.

"Muse Upon Missing Thee"

The lustrous light shines dimly tonight
for truth of our distant hands.
The soft summer smiles have taken
wings in favor of sadness in my heart.
This, I say, is far too great a price to pay
for one who would verily throw all else away,
just to be in your presence,
touching my place in the world.
By your side, I am at home and alive.
There, my spirit is boundless, without form.
The wine from my chalice flows from all that I am,
and I want for nothing beyond
what is in and of you.
I am drawn to you, as the moth
to the flame, basking
in the light and warmth of your
essence, celebrating
my existence and the profoundly
exquisite experience
that is birthed from our touch. I
have but one passion
to give, but it is all that I am. My
love is unending for you
and I give it freely, forever.
But tonight I muse upon missing thee.

"Muted Query"

A query quivers upon thy lips,
Pensive, behind thine eyes,
Begging the blue of thy briny seas,
Wherein this wanting lies.

In passing hither, I noted thence,
A marveling within thy orbs,
Which doth they secret thoughts belie,
And doth my glance absorb.

It speaks so clearly, without a word,
This transient, wanting thought,
But in thy soul doth linger long,
And beg thy lips speak soft.

But fear consigns this query o'er.
And binds thy muted tongue,
That in thy orbs this wanting lay,
In depths, til time is gone.

"My Hunger State"

This ol' state is Texas hell,
   In days beyond your leave,
On mesas flat and gullies dry,
    There blows an ill felt breeze.

That browns the barren pastures barbed,
   In dusty devils hell,
And choke so dry the tears I cry,
    That would the ground befell.

How plea we thee your feet to tread,
    Again the trail this gate?
That lilac sweet upon the air,
   Would sate my hunger state.

And once again make green that grow,
   Within my heart this thing,
For nest thee well the whippoorwill,
   That in my meadow sing.

"My Resting Place"

Give me not an earthen stone,
To mark my resting place,
But in thy heart a cozy nest,
That wilst my love embrace.

Take me in thy most seclude,
And all of time we'll own.
Our love there soft and warmly be,
Unlike the earthen stone.

Give me life in thy breast,
As my resting place,
That I know not the dark discard,
Of a berth with a stony face.

Hold me in thy heart so true,
That I might ever live,
Whither travel that thy might,
My spirit, ever captive.

"Obsession"

How else I measure, that in my heart,
My deep devotion to thee?
By words and deeds of lesser thought,
Or outright fantasy?
How does one know beyond a doubt,
The count of heartbeats true,
That fill my cup of life each day,
Which overfloweth with you?
How oft my thoughts throughout the day,
Do spiral into thee,
Which lead me to that fluid state,
Of doubtful sanity.
How doth I know this realm is real,
And all therein be true,
Lest there I find the same in heart,
Of me inside of you?
How wilst I say "I want to live",
In truthful words with passion,
Lest I be true to you in me,
My love, my one obsession.

"Neglect"

Neglect is such an ugly word,
Connoting ruinous fray.
Dank and musty doth it smell,
Odious in every way.

Reeking of shallow rooted love,
That reach not to the core,
Causing one to question false,
A truth thy must abhor.

Neglect is such an ugly word,
Rancorous of cowardly way,
A rancid act of friendship not,
Which doth the bond decay.

"Ocean Within"

I pray for the spirit of he who never ventured
beyond the security of the shoreline of life
fearing the depths of the ocean within.
Few things are so empty as a life
void of trust and faith.
The ocean within is vast, deep
and, at times, perilous.
But sailing it defines us, changing us for the good.
Trust and faith make for a worthy ship.
To carry an unsailed epithet to the grave
is indeed evidence of a wasted life.
Nothing is so empty as a spirit
moored at the shore,
Anchored in fear of the ocean within.
And no one is more alive than
he who has sailed once,
that ocean, and know the depths of true love.

"Ode to Micayla's Sleep"

I shall neither know deeper satisfaction,
Nor greater presence of mind
than that of awakening,
To sight and sound of Micayla, breathing soft,
Nestled upon my chest with tiny hands touching
My very soul, as only she can while she sleeps.
The experience is beyond the brush of an artist,
And fleet well from capture by eloquent poets.
Our love speaks directly in our hearts,
Sharing naught with the world
our quiescent words.

About this poem: Micayla is my three year old granddaughter who speaks to my heart with love and total trust when she climbs on my lap and takes her nap. I usually nap as our hearts speak to each, words that no one hears but us.

"Of My Youthful Yesterday"

In the still of my moments,
Within eddies of wayward thoughts,
The vividly painful images there,
Haunt that my youth has wrought.
The look across the pond of time,
Gives way to introspect,
And grieves the elder man in me,
For lack of then intellect.
I drift a time amid debris,
Of yesterday in our thought,
And note the time given then,
To that which I mighten'd ought.
I burned the days of my youth,
With reckless darkened fright,
With no regard for what the cost
And consequence it might.
But save from me did time itself,
The gift I am today,
And freed me from the dauntless grip,
Of my youthful yesterday.

"Portend"

The songbirds sing ever so sweet,
While lilies dance in the wind,
There, on a hillside in the midst of thee,
Is the love this verse portends.

A friend who finds your loving eyes,
There, in all he sees,
Holds your heart in high regard,
That thee with he be pleased.

Ever present in all our moments,
In every heartbeat and breath,
Never more than a whisper away,
Even into the dark of death.

No song so sweet as that of thee,
No fragrance wafts as *your* winds,
No silence ever tween our thoughts,
Our love this verse portends.

"Ready That I"

Ready that I move on,
To realms beyond the pain,
Where days know not the dark of night,
And eyes not know the rain.

Ready that I take flight,
On wings in clouds of joy,
To suffer not of carnal woes,
And bind beyond of Roy.

Ready that I be free to live,
And cast away this hell.
Too cold I think a loveless life,
Beyond my lips could tell.

Ready that I tread the path,
A final trail this life,
And rest asleep the tortured thoughts,
Of angst, beguiled and writhe.

Ready that I look upon the Son,
To wash his feet my sins,
And find my name upon the list,
Of golden gate let in.

"Seasons"

The days of chaste snow and youth
Blanket the reality of life's woe.
But time sets about its journey full,
As spring doth swiftly come and go.

Ceding to summer's primal urge,
Set in motion in past milleniums,
That oft boil the very blood
Of passion for life within us.

Too swiftly we turn autumn's page,
In pale thought of tomorrow,
That usher thence frigid realities
Of winter's bitter sorrow.

Alas, the leaves celebrate their freedom
To go wither the tree cannot.
And the winds of time abet them,
Scraping across life's frozen lot.

"Spirit Of An Old Oak"

Under a gnarly old oak, upon a lonely rise,
With disfigured limbs, barren of memories,
Sits there a spirit, waning, longing
For the leaflets of its extremities.

But the winds of time have scattered them hither,
Fleeting echoes of the existence,
Of a once vibrant arbor,
Where the spirit now bares witness.

Even the birds forsake it,
As unfitting the gaiety of their song,
And once cool, jostling breeze,
Amidst barren branches, have gone.

The rooted taps that once drew life,
And drank from deep rivers sweet,
Now as arid anchors rest,
And serve as stony feet.

The sanguine sun sets dusty low,
On images fair gone by,
As death's arid winds sickle o'er,
Taunting the spirit to die.

The darkened winds now swirl to claim,
The gnarly remnants there,
But the spirit keeps naught with vapid nights,
That cloak it's bygone lair.

"Tears O' My Soul"

I lie silently upon my thoughts of tomorrow
listening to the rain of tears dripping
from the edge of my pain.
I count the heartaches, pulsing, as my arms
ache to be filled again with the joy of you.
Sometimes, my tears cascade from somewhere
deep in my soul and my breath drowns
with agonizing pleas for your voice, touch
or anything of you to let me know that I
am still alive and worthy of the air I breath.
My life is incomplete without you and
tomorrow's sunrise will never be as sweet
as when it finally rises in our eyes
as we peer deep into each other's soul.

"The Gift"

Fragile be, the gift called love,
Delicate, wispy and lite,
But vapor in possessive hearts,
When therein held too tight.
A lacy veil on feathered time,
It seeks a heart that's free,
But fleet from being held too fast,
Effacing which would be.
Delicate, yet endurant,
Ever present on the shores of time,
It ebbs and flows in hearts genteel,
As that of sanguine wine.
Seek not possession of the gift,
Hold fast to this behest,
Yield ye to the gift instead,
And by it... be possessed.

"The Last Poem"

Last night I dreamt a chamber white,
With nary a seat within,
Its luminous walls, tall and bright,
And sins of my life therein.

They lay at my feet, as leaves of my tree,
Distinct, yet pallidly white,
Marked as my own, faint shadowy they,
Their origins, dark as the night.

My sins and I, reviewed the lie,
A life that had brought us there,
No window's sight, the porte fast tight,
Just walls and floor and air.

Then quickly did yield, my blackened soul,
Purging my fears to the light,
Swiftly transcending the upper plane,
Of pure and righteously right.

Beyond the room lie infinite peace,
An ease I had never known,
My sins forgiven, on the floor there lay,
As my Father had called me home.

About this poem: This work actually relates a dream that I had regarding my death and subsequent experience of being cleansed of my sins and accepted by God as worthy of His Kingdom.

"The Sparrow's Song"

What if the sparrow never sang for her sunrise,
and horizons ached for a single sunset?
What if all that happened between were reduced
to simple terms yielding a flavorless existence?
What if perception were not as worthy
as the reality that lay before us?
How many tortured moments would you count
on the wayward path which lead not by the brook?
Who amongst us has the courage
to lift up a bowed
head to the Universal Spirit and look upon truth
with both open eyes and heart?
And what about It's lessons of unconditional love,
Which, at any moment, could
be our salvation except
for some twisted need we have for control?
Hope is best known as a little place in Arkansas.
And the winds weep for want
of the sparrow's song.

"Theo Egan"

Serene, by the river,
Like the water, she flows,
Slowly, deeply in our souls,
Touching us as she goes.
Her memory, like a symphony,
Her wind as a bow,
Across the strings of our hearts,
She plays us soft and slow.
Along the river Spokane,
Our loving patron gives,
And in each note of our score,
Theo Egan lives.
She lives as a symphony,
That plays upon our hearts,
In perfect pitch with the river time,
In us, she's always a part.
One by one, we all join in,
To hold her loving hand,
And flow the score on the river slow,
With Theo Egan again.

"To Be Thy Valentine"

I fancy the magic in your eyes,
    And court that thy heart truly speaks.
    Of unmasked candor my soul doth seek,
To know the depths in thy heart I lie.
And win the thoughts of pure delight,
    When muse you in the winds,
    To know the day replete with friend,
Of lustrous golden light.
To hold that moment in rapture fine,
    And bind of me to thee,
        I trade my heart and all therein,
To be thy valentine.
    And beg the winds to set we free,
        For love of two true friends.

"Uncommon Girl"

Amongst the stones, the riverbed I
Did find a gem, a pearl.
The luminous glow in eyes, a glint,
I marvel uncommon girl.

Glimmering slow in shifting light,
Her beauty beyond the pale.
Of want possess the glow therein,
Did I the bed assail.

Then rend free the lustrous pearl,
To fill my night and day,
And add the glow its loving light,
To that of cold and gray.

And yield the flow serenely black,
A commonly unlit stream,
But fired my passion evermore,
Uncommon girl of my dreams.

"Unfinished"

Unfinished lyrics to an unfinished song,
The birds quit their own spirit,
Abstaining, foregoing the need
To revel the dawning day.

Unfinished journey unto that land,
Of long sought promise and bliss,
For retreat into yesterday,
And the comfort of a well-worn path.

Unfinished promises lying about,
Empty of purpose and direction,
But validly hinged upon hope,
That fulfillment bind their reality.

Unfinished dreams, hauntingly awake,
With no quarter for the weary mind,
That seek not tempest nor final rest,
But simply to finish the unfinished.

About this poem: There are regrettable things in our pasts that haunt us, begging for completion and rest.

"Unkind Time"

I peered into your window once,
And all that I could see,
Were faded wispy images,
Of days that use to be.

Confused, I stood in wonder,
To contemplate your haste,
Yet urged me did you in my thoughts,
What's left of thee not waste.

But in my way, I stopped to marvel,
My wondrously precious foe,
That giveth sunshine on my face,
Yet seek to press me low.

And ask of thee did I at once,
To know thy moody blade,
That places upon my heart such mirth,
Yet rend to the bloody glade.

And spake ye not in any terms,
The queries of my pages,
But yield my face and hands to gray,
A mere footnote of the ages.

"Unshadowed"

The dense umbra that gloom my essence,
Without announcement, is flooded,
From all angles by a luminesce presence,
The likes of which is unknown.
Consumed, in a moment of ecstacy,
I yield all that I know me to be,
Trembling, quite expectantly,
As I bask in her strength and beauty.
Suddenly, all becomes clear,
As with the loss of darkness.
My redefinition rises from my fear.
Even my shadow is vanquished.
In the after stillness, my liberator stands
Over my defeated yesterdays,
Lighting tomorrow as only she can,
Unifying my spirit with peace and courage.
That I am today bear naught
Of he and noted shadows yore,
I have passed in an instance of thought,
From thence to un-shadowed, and my hero is she.

"Unspoken"

Unspoken, the fleeting thoughts
that pass between our eyes,
where we share glances, behind hearts
as shields, from across the distance.
And yet, in these eyes are words,
begging for eloquent airing,
to breath the bouquet
of our quiet imaginings.
Perhaps a question that lingers long
might find its way to light
and know the answer to itself.
What lies beyond these hearts,
and indeed, these eyes
that glance and fleet on small passings
across the gulf of unspoken?
Perhaps our imaginings are not
So very far apart, that bliss
could be born thereto
as a bridge across this gulf.
But alas, we may never know with clarity
what truths there lay in eyes,
that in their passing, give curtsy and bow
to fleeting thoughts that we leave, unspoken.

"Wave Upon Wave"

Your love comes over me, like a blanket
Of warm, wind driven surf,
Wave upon wave, unending, yet gentle,
Rinsing away my hurt.

It feels of soothing sea breeze,
That gently stir my soul,
Caressing soft my spirit there,
Making of me, a human whole.

That I am given to feel of thee,
On the shores of my psyche and soul,
Is to know at end my place in life,
As in my heart, I thee hold.

"Wherein The Silence Rains"

Silence harbors glimpses,
Of moments lost in time,
That ever rain relentless on,
In waking states of mind.

Sleep doth hold a measure count,
Of freedom from the rain,
Yet even so, it therein roars,
And write the soul with pain.

Angst engulf the visions there,
The islet serenities,
That fleet on fearful passage by,
The fractured sanities.

And of the dark that holds the calm,
With space not 'tween of twain,
Oust the songs o'the meadowlark,
Wherein the silence rains.

"While You Sleep"

In moments like this, I treat myself to
tender thoughts of your smile warming
my heart, your wispy touch, and the
indescribable joy of laying next to you
while you sleep, listening to you breath.
I have found in my soul, no place so peaceful
than the comforting warmth of our love.
There is something so incredibly right about
you in me. I often find myself consumed
with the idea that I can somehow capture
these feelings in verse and give them to you
as a precious gift. But alas, my pen will not obey
my heart. And I am left to anticipate your eyes
awakening so that I can look my love deep
into your soul again and see it
reflect back into mine.
Until then, I am content to guard your
every breath with this profound love in my heart.
I belong to you Baby...completely...forever.
And I pray to always know the
indescribable joy of
watching you while you sleep.

"Yearning Thee"

Yearning thee opens my soul,
As a wound for all to see,
Exposing full, therein defined,
The abyss that inhabits me.
Yet, each day I embrace the pain,
For it is all that I have left.
I grieve the utter emptiness,
For knowledge of thee bereft.
And questions lay o'my nature true,
Once strength, for the moment, 'tis inert,
Laid aside, rendered null,
In the void of this darkened dearth.

"Evidence Of My Presence"

Ravages o'er the march of time,
Cannot these words conceal,
As willst the flesh in time entomb.
And rob my youthful zeal.
My words know not quiescent tombs,
Nor waning moment's kind,
They live in perpetuity, free,
In currents on the river time.
Their port, my soul, as birthing womb,
Imbue their spirit free,
Passing through this mortal port,
To bind with eternity.
In these words, are there ensconced,
Vignettes of my mortal essence,
Lingering e'er on the river time,
As evidence of my presence.

Thank You
For Reading
Our Story

To Our Readers

Thank you for reading our story. I hope you enjoyed reading it as much as we did living it.

You may be wondering how our story continued. Luster and I both found our way back to one another, became even better friends and were married on September 16th, 2008. We lived a blissful life, however the river of life continued to give us some unchartered rapids. Luster suffered a stroke the day after Christmas in 2011. While he recovered well from it, he was soon after diagnosed with prostate cancer. We lived with this unwelcome intruder in our lives until April 19, 2019. We couldn't have scripted a better day for the Lord to call him home. The door was open, there was a slight breeze, the redbirds were singing and we were together.

Luster wrote our story along with his poetry in hopes that it would one day be published. Life has a way of taking its own path. While we were unable to accomplish this in his lifetime, he left me his treasured gift to share with all whose lives our story may touch. It is my honor and with great pleasure to share his eloquent words, and his kind, loving and romantic heart.

Marilyn K. Lewis

www.ingramcontent.com/pod-product-compliance
Lightning Source LLC
Chambersburg PA
CBHW071206070526
44584CB00019B/2930